SEP 1980

RECEIVED
OHIO DOMINICAN
COLLEGE LIBRARY
COLUMBUS, OHIO
43219

W9-BCI-764

TWAYNE'S WORLD AUTHORS SERIES
A Survey of the World's Literature

HUNGARY

Enikö Molnár Basa, American University

EDITOR

Mihály Vitéz Csokonai

TWAS 579

Csokonai Vitéz Mihály.

MIHÁLY VITÉZ CSOKONAI

By ANNA B. KATONA

College of Charleston

TWAYNE PUBLISHERS

A DIVISION OF G. K. HALL & CO., BOSTON

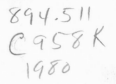

894.511
C958K
1980

Copyright © 1980 by G. K. Hall & Co.

Published in 1980 by Twayne Publishers,
A Division of G. K. Hall & Co.
All Rights Reserved

Printed on permanent/durable acid-free paper and bound
in the United States of America

First Printing

Frontispiece of Mihály Vitéz Csokonai

reproduced from the collection of the Library of Congress.

Library of Congress Cataloging in Publication Data

Katona, Anna.
Mihály Vitéz Csokonai.

(Twayne's world authors series; TWAS 579: Hungary)
Bibliography: p. 161–64
Includes index.
1.   Csokonai Vitéz, Mihály, 1773–1805
Criticism and interpretation
PH3194.C8Z725   894'.511'11   79-24091
ISBN 0-8057-6421-6

To my native city and my *alma mater*:
Csokonai's Debrecen and College

111594

Contents

About the Author

Anna B. Katona was born on July 7, 1920 in Debrecen, Hungary. She earned a Ph. D. from the University of Debrecen and a post-doctoral degree from the Hungarian Academy of Sciences. She was the chairman of the English Department at the University of Debrecen and is presently Professor of English at the College of Charleston. She had two British Council scholarships, a Ford Foundation grant, an American Council of Learned Societies grant and served twice on the ACLS European Screening Committee as well as a trustee in the Dickens Society. For sometime she edited "Hungarian Studies in English," a publication of the University of Debrecen. She wrote numerous articles, on English and American literatures, on Hungary's cultural ties with those countries, for Hungarian, English and Canadian-American publications. She also published a book on George Eliot, co-authored a history of English literature and edited *A Casebook on the United States*, the first such book in Hungary.

Preface

It has been a challenge to write this first English book on one of Hungary's greatest poets. I had in mind an audience that has had no opportunity so far to read Csokonai's enchanting poetry and most probably has not even heard of him. In consequence, the presentation had to be informative and comprehensive. As always, personal preferences have influenced the selection of poems interpreted, but most of the great poems found in all anthologies are included. Because of the nearly insurmountable language barrier, my task has often been frustrating. Magyar is a Finno-Ugrian language, differing radically from Indo-European languages in its grammatical structure and unrelated to them in its vocabulary; the nature of the language, combined with Csokonai's exceptional virtuosity in creating visual and sound effects, makes an adequate English version almost impossible. To this should be added the many unavoidable terms to which no English equivalents exist, since the phenomena they describe are unknown in the English-speaking world. Even the poet's name presents a problem: Csokonai Vitéz, Mihály (Michael), according to the Library of Congress catalog, a multiple surname. As a matter of fact, Vitéz is the poet's true surname. Csokonai simply indicates that the family came from the village Csokonya. However, the poet consistently referred to himself as Csokonai, and it is by this name that he is known in Hungarian literature. There is no satisfactory English version; I have chosen the form Mihály Vitéz Csokonai, rather than Mihály Csokonai Vitéz, because it will help the English-speaking reader identify the poet in a more proper way.

Csokonai disregarded chronology in the arrangement of his own works for publication and he rewrote most of his poems so frequently that it is not always easy to categorize them in terms of time. In view of this fact, instead of the chronological order generally followed in monographs on Csokonai, this critical-analytical discussion is arranged by themes. It seemed appropriate to follow the background introduction by a chapter on the most remarkable feature of his art, his eclecticism. There is a curious mixture of styles in Csokonai's poems, in which the baroque, mannerism, classicism, rococo, sentimentalism, and some romantic features, enriched with elements of folklore, appear simultaneously. Csokonai's determination to raise Hungary's cultural level makes a chapter on his theoretical essays and on his genre-creating activity indispensable; this chapter also prepares the way for the discussion of the poet's political views. The unending controversy over Csokonai's changing opinions necessitated special consideration of this delicate issue. The last two chapters deal with the poet's major achievements: his philosophical verse and his love poetry. In the present monograph, the former category is not limited to the conventional approach, and besides the so-called great poems of the Enlightenment it also includes various poems relating to the poet's philosophy of life.

Csokonai (1773–1805) would have loved to be part of a World Authors series. Not only did Hungarian literature first attain European standards with his brief career, not only is he the first poet of world literary status in the language, but also in backward Hungary, he had a vision and understanding of world literature at a time when such a concept was first recognized by Goethe. This book, then, addresses itself both to the average reader and to today's comparatists in particular. To scholars in comparative studies, Csokonai offers a key to the better understanding of problems involving the mixture of various cultures. Throughout the centuries, Hungarians have been kinless in an ocean of surrounding Germans and Slavs, attached to their very different heritage, but at the same time eager to assimilate Western civilization. They have seen their country, "set," as Csokonai put it, "between comely west and rough east,"— a kind of bridge. The poet himself is such a bridge; in his writings and language West-European refinement merged with the down-to-earth character of contemporary Hungarian letters and produced a poetry that in many of its aspects surprises us with its modernity. By fully assimilating the totality of contemporary Western culture and transplanting it onto Hungarian soil, he created a poetry of special flavor and unique character. It is frequently remarked of the famous Hungarian wine that there would be no Tokay without the vine imported from abroad, yet the Hungarian soil transformed it into something special, unmatched anywhere else. The same principle applies to the best of Hungarian literature and to Csokonai. He assimilated all the various trends and styles; imitated all the Italian, German, English, and French models. But they all turned into something entirely different in his hand; they acquired a peculiar, unmatched flavor in the special

Hungarian environment through the medium of that Magyar language Csokonai elevated and refined to perfection.

In our age, with the increasing awareness of mankind's cultural variety, the study of Csokonai is most rewarding for critics interested in comparative studies. For their benefit, this analysis will offer constant references to Western parallels. It will also repeatedly point out the adversities that befell this unfortunate poet, not only because these misfortunes strongly influenced his writings, but mostly because they are symbolic of the Hungarian national predicament and in consequence, indispensable to the understanding of Magyar culture. Finally, whenever possible, there will be emphasis on Csokonai's modernity, the fact that the poetry of a crisis-ridden poet in a crisis-ridden period of his nation's history has a special relevance in this crisis-ridden twentieth century.

The prose translations of his poems here presented emphasize the use of figurative language. No attempt has been made to render meter, rhythm, or rhyme. At their most successful, these English renderings will recreate the unique atmosphere of Csokonai's gently hurting poetry. His was and is a tragic fate. Amid adverse conditions, without due recognition, frustrated Csokonai, the greatest Magyar poet of his time, was "dreaming of the twentieth century." Unfortunately, in the twentieth century, Csokonai, this pioneer of world literature, has still no place in world literature because of the language barrier. If this critical-analytical presentation will help the reader to share in a new experience, if this monograph will provide a flickering insight into a hitherto unknown area of world literature, if it will awaken the reader's curiosity about Csokonai and Magyar culture, my work of love, this book on the greatest poet of my native city, will be amply rewarded.

Anna B. Katona

College of Charleston

Acknowledgments

For the permission to quote from Csokonai's work I am indebted to Szépirodalmi Kiadó. I also want to acknowledge the permission by Carcanet Press Limited to quote from Thomas Crawford's anthology, *Love, Labour and Liberty: the eighteenth-century Scottish lyric*. To Mrs. Lewis Mumford and to Dr. Thomas Tenney I wish to express my sincerest gratitude for reading the manuscript in its initial stages. Very special thanks go to Paul Allen who has worked with me for months on the English prose-versions of Csokonai's poems. I also wish to thank the College of Charleston for reducing my teaching load for one term so that I had more time to work on this book. My warmest thanks go to former students, all in different walks of life, but all close to Csokonai in more than one way, and without whose help this monograph could not have been written.

Chronology

1773   November 17, Mihály Vitéz Csokonai born in Debrecen.

1780   Enters the College of Debrecen, an institution providing elementary, secondary, and higher education.

1785   Writes first poems as school exercises.

1786   Father dies; their fortune is lost.

1791   Writes *Békaegérharc*.

1793   Writes *Tempefői*; first poem published in the *Magyar Hírmondó*.

1794–   Teaching assistant of the poetry class at the College of Deb-
1795   recen; publishes a list of his works in the *Magyar Hírmondó*; the same periodical publishes the first critical appraisal of his activity; writes his great philosophical poems and a pastoral novel.

1795   February 28, his play *Gerson du malheureux* is performed at the college. March, the *Uránia* publishes four of his poems. May 20, in Pest at the time of the Martinovics executions. June 15, farewell address to the students of the College of Debrecen. June 20, expelled from the college as a result of a lengthy disciplinary procedure (1794–1795). Studies law at the College of Sárospatak.

1796   Summer, a guest of Ádám Horváth Pálóczi (in its structure this name is similar to that of Csokonai) in Balatonfüred, he writes the first version of "A tihanyi ekhóhoz." November–December, in Pozsony (Bratislava) he publishes the versified newspaper *A Diétai Magyar Múzsa*.

1797   Summer, in Komárom he falls in love with Júlia Vajda.

1798   Fails to get a teaching job at the Georgikon, an agricultural college in Keszthely, the first in the country. March, writes his farewell letter to Júlia after her marriage to a merchant. Moves to County Somogy where he stays with friends. Summer, in Kisasszod, he writes "A magánossághoz."

1799   Finishes *Dorottya*; takes up a teaching job in Csurgó. His students perform his plays *Cultura* and *Az özvegy Karnyóné*.

1800   February, leaves Csurgó; July, returns to Debrecen on foot and penniless to live in his mother's house. His poem "A szépség ereje a bajnoki szíven" appears as an independent booklet; he organizes his poems for publication and works on his unfinished epic, *Árpád*.

1801   His plan to edit the *Magyar Hírmondó* in Vienna fails.

1802   His translation of Ewald Kleist's poem is published as "A tavasz"; he is refused a job at the National Library founded at that time by the Count Széchenyi; July 11, the Great Fire destroys part of the College of Debrecen and a thousand houses, among them that of Csokonai's mother.

1803   His volume *Anakreoni dalok* is printed in Vienna but it will appear only in 1806. His poems "A pillangóhóz," "A reményhez," and "Szemrehányás" are published with musical notations.

1804   *Dorottya* is published. April 15, at the funeral of the Countess Rhédey in Nagyvárad (Oradea) he reads his poem "Halotti versek." April 22, returns to Debrecen sick with pneumonia; June, "Halotti versek" is published without the poet's knowledge in a mutilated version.

1805   Dies on January 28; buried on January 29. His *Lilla, érzékeny dalok három könyvben, Ódák két könyvben*, and *Alkalmatosságra írt versek*, prepared by him for publication, are published after his death.

1813   The first edition of his collected works, *Csokonai Vitéz Mihály poétai munkái*, appears in four volumes in Vienna.

CHAPTER 1

Roots

I *Europe, Hungary, and Csokonai*

PREACHERS are like candles; they burn and give light to all; are useful to all, but in the process they consume themselves. This description of Protestant ministers in sixteenth-century Hungary applies well to Csokonai's predicament. The most outstanding Hungarian poet of his time, eager to elevate his backward country to a European level, he has been a strong influence on Magyar poetry well into the twentieth century. Candles and lights fit the central imagery of the Age of the Enlightenment whose ideas he propagated, and of the poet himself. Born in 1773, until his early death in 1805, throughout his brief life spanning this most revolutionary period in human history—the American Revolution and the French Revolution—Csokonai was "consumed" by public and private misfortunes, hectic work, and tuberculosis. His life and career were shaped by circumstances of the contemporary Hungarian scene.[1]

After the devastating one hundred and fifty year Turkish occupation of much of the country, Hungary was faced in the eighteenth century with a painful new beginning under unfavorable conditions. Not only was part of the country a depopulated wasteland, not only was the whole country, economically, socially, and culturally backward, but in addition, the Habsburgs tried to keep it a food and raw material producing colony of Austria. As Csokonai so emphatically explained in a letter to Count Széchenyi: "In proximity to so many bright nations we conduct our lives as if we still lived in tents on the Caspean shores. Close to the end of this enlightened century, for us the unhappy medieval times still seem to continue" (II, 832). And yet, change, though slow and barely distinguishable, was under way. Under the growing influence of the radical ideas reaching Hungary through Vienna from France, political and cultural activity intensified in the second half of the century. That movement for national

15

independence and democratic progress which culminated almost a century later in the War of Independence of 1848–1849, started sometime around 1770. Indeed, the most significant impact of the French Enlightenment, in Hungary and elsewhere in Eastern Europe, was to make people aware of their national backwardness and to make them realize the importance of social progress. The chaos and confusion of the troubled nation almost resist clarification: national independence and democratic progress were the main issues, but there was a complete disagreement on priorities. Radical intellectuals were dedicated to the ideas of the French Enlightenment and to democratic reforms for everyone in the nation. The estates, considering themselves the nation and callously disregarding the rest of the population, sought freedom and equality for nobles only; they were most unwilling to give up their vested interest in a quasi-feudal economy. At the same time, their fight for their "ancient" privileges and for local autonomy coincided with the struggle for national liberation. The nobility and the radicals could seldom see eye to eye about priorities: whether to become a humanitarian or a patriot became a torturing dilemma for the most outstanding minds.

When Emperor Joseph II (1780–1790), an enlightened absolute monarch, attempted the introduction of progressive reforms, he made the serious mistake of disregarding circumstances peculiar to Hungary. By insisting on the use of German, he offended national pride and alienated the estates altogether. The collective fear for the survival of the nation in a German-Slavonic environment prompted a resistance which around the year 1790 succeeded for a brief period in reaching a singular coalition of the nobility with radical forces. It was at this time—when Csokonai was attaining adulthood—that the vernacular, this vehicle of national culture, became the key issue. Later, poets came to be recognized as standard-bearers of ideas of progress. This peculiar role of the poets in Hungary and in most of Eastern Europe, as leaders of the nation in the struggle for independence and for progress, is unconceivable in Western Europe. In Hungary, the assertion of cultural identity was the first step in a long political struggle. With Csokonai, literature in Magyar, for the first time, attained European standards. Astonishingly, his career coincided with a period of literary vacuum in the country at large. Beginning in 1772, a literary revival inspired great expectations for further development for meaningful cultural activity, but unfortunately, that budding literary life was brought to an abrupt end in 1795, after the disclosure of the so-called Martinovics conspiracy (its leader was

Ignác Martinovics), a frustrated and poorly organized attempt at radical changes inspired by the French Revolution. The poets were brutally silenced, either by execution or by long prison terms; the shadow of suspicion was cast on all activities in Hungarian and on any association with ideas from abroad. Even earlier, a French spy hunt had alarmed the country. An English traveler, Robert Townson, visiting Hungary in 1793, recalled having been suspected of bearing a false English passport as a cover-up for allegedly propagating pernicious French ideas.[2]

It was in such circumstances that Csokonai emerged on the literary scene.

II *From Debrecen to Debrecen*

Csokonai was born in Debrecen on November 17, 1773, a month before the Boston Tea Party, the son of József Csokonai, a barber-surgeon with an eminent training in Latin and in natural sciences, an admirer of Ferenc Rákóczi, the leader of the defeated so-called "kuruc" anti-Habsburg insurgence (1705–1711) and a supporter of Emperor Joseph's reforms, and of Sára Diószegi, daughter of a respected citizen, a furrier.[3] A woman with an education above her state, she read to her two sons Fénelon's *Télémaque*, a novel that epitomized the philosophy of the Enlightenment. Csokonai was four when he learnt to read and write. He entered the College of Debrecen in 1780. His father died in 1786 leaving the family penniless. In 1793 Csokonai had his first poem published, and the next year he became a teaching assistant in charge of the poetry class. With this he had attained the peak of his security. Indeed, in the future he was to have no security whatsoever in any sense of the word. During this short period of stability he wrote, besides minor verse, his great philosophical poems of the Enlightenment, a mock-epic, a pastoral novel, and two dramas.

In 1795, the year of the disclosure of the Martinovics conspiracy, he was expelled from the college—according to the minutes—for offending college rules. He then transferred to Sárospatak to study law at the college there. Law did not satisfy him, so he left. In 1796 we find him in Pozsony (Bratislava) trying to find patrons among the estates assembled there for the diet, with a versified newspaper—an unsuccessful venture. In 1797 he moved to Komárom where, at the king's call, the nobility gathered in preparation for the fight against the French. It was in Komárom that Csokonai fell in love with Júlia

18   MIHÁLY VITÉZ CSOKONAI

Vajda, the daughter of a well-to-do grain merchant, but Júlia married a merchant instead, and a disillusioned Csokonai wandered all around Transdanubia, mostly in county Somogy, enjoying the hospitality of friends and for a short time teaching in Csurgó. Many of his mature love poems, some with philosophical connotations, the mock-epic *Dorottya*, and two more dramas belong to this period. In Csurgó Csokonai eked out a meager existence, without fuel in winter, without a candle at night, and without a decent attire for the examination performances. No wonder he decided to return to his native Debrecen. As his poem "Visszajövetel az Alföldről" ("On Returning from the Alföld") shows he was homesick, heartbroken, and longing to be back to Debrecen's "friendly smoke" and "the home-land's winds."

Hectic and frustrating years followed his return in 1800, when he tried without success to get a job and to publish his works. Some delightful, gently sorrowful poems as well as his longest philosophical poem are the products of those last years which he spent in his mother's tiny house. The quiet peacefulness of this Debrecen Rousseau, as he saw himself, was destroyed by the Great Fire of 1802: "That tiny abode too and that tiny garden, which for me served as Tuscullanum, became a victim of the catastrophe. I am writing these lines midst black rust and ashes. Between heaven, that did not commiserate with me, and myself, whom it deprived even of this little, there is nothing but a thin board that cannot protect me even from rain. Even now the wind is strewing my own and my neighbor's flying ashes on this sad letter through my burnt-out windows" (II, 903). This letter to a friend was one of several in which the poet asked for financial help. He died in 1805, a disillusioned man. There on Debrecen's "prairie of loneliness," in the beginning of "the Hungarian age of Hope," "he was in his country the most outcast fugitive person," in the words of his fellow-poets Árpád Tóth and Endre Ady respectively.

To this brief biography a short character sketch should be added. A hypersensitive, rather shy, and private person, somewhat of an adolescent all his life, Csokonai was at the same time fond of company and liked to hide his shyness behind spectacular action. He was a man of extremes: "French fever and English cold-blood mixed in me"—he said (II, 975). No category will hold a phenomenon of such stature. He defies definition as much as does his native Debrecen. As his first biographer, a former student said: "it is impossible to know him since his soul is unmeasurable." [4] The poet Ady thus summed up the confusing contradictions of that phenomenon that was Csokonai: "He was a reveler, a tramp, uncouth, coarse, and boorish. As a matter of fact, he was in his time the most European person in this country." [5] This perturbed spirit was overpowered by the desperately complicated issues of his country, which, coupled with his personal misfortunes, never gave him a moment of relief after his exile from the college.

He died in January, 1805, only a few months after Napoleon's coronation as emperor. Besides the American Revolution and the French Revolution, that period also witnessed the beginning of the Industrial Revolution in England. Indeed, the foundations of our modern world were laid during our poet's short life. No wonder his poetry strikes us as so modern. He not only raised his native literature to European standards in the then current classical trend, but, transcending this impersonal public poetry, he introduced the new personal mode that was to dominate the Romantic Age. In the early twentieth century, Ady, the father of modern Hungarian lyric and his circle admired Csokonai; they admired this son of feudal Hungary, this Calvinistic Hungarian reading Voltaire, engaged in a feverish siege of the West. [6] If it seems that such a characterization is paradoxical, we must bear in mind that there is no end to the striking paradoxes in our poet's life and career. Csokonai's real achievements consist in a wonderful synthesis of what seems to be mutually exclusive opposites.

This most musical poet of Hungary had never heard a first rate concert all his life. This ardent pioneer of Hungarian drama never saw a respectable theatrical performance. This learned poet had to spend many years among friends who, though well-meaning, could neither share nor understand his concerns and among whom he lacked the thought-provoking intercourse of peers. Born in the easternmost part of the country, he was the most westernized intellectual of the age, but at the same time the most Magyar. He was a lonely figure, not only because of the adverse political situation that left the young emerging poet alone on the cultural scene, but above all, because his understanding of the discrepancy between Hungary's backwardness and Western Europe's culture was so great that none of his compatriots could grasp it. This explains his terrifying isolation. A furiously active and impatient man, he was continually making inordinate demands on the backward world around him. Poetry was his sole companion. His understanding of Hungary's real situation was matched only by his ability to span and bridge the gap between Hungary and Europe in poetry. By uniting the racy local color of his native Debrecen with learning and refinement on the European level, he became a characteristically Magyar poet with a European perspective. This brings us to the issue of Debrecen. Some knowledge about this most controversial city will be necessary for the better understanding of its greatest poet.

III   Debrecen and Csokonai

Debrecen is more than a geographical point on the map in easternmost Hungary; Debrecen is a state of mind which none but a native of the city really understands and which nobody has ever successfully explained. It is a state of mind that eludes definition.[7] The phoenix in the city's arms symbolizes the incredible resilience and tenacity of this settlement, built—to the amazement of the Englishman Townson—far from ocean, river, or other geographical location that would normally justify the planning of a city. "To what circumstances Debritzin owes its existence I don't know"—he wrote when he visited there in May, 1793—"nor can I divine what can have induced thirty thousand people to select a country destitute of springs, rivers, building materials, fuel and the heart-cheering vine for their residence." With its inhabitants of "gloomy manners and dress," this place, which he called "perhaps the greatest village in Europe," remained a mystery to him.[8] Lonely Debrecen in the very heart of the desolate Hungarian plainland is almost the perfect symbol of the kinless Hungarian nation in the midst of Germans and Slavs. In a country that had only six settlements with a population of over 20,000, in 1787, Debrecen, with its 25,748 inhabitants was the second largest city after Pozsony (Bratislava) where the diets were held. And yet Townson was right in calling it a village. Even small West-European towns had an urban character with a population differing in occupation and lifestyle from those in the countryside. Well into the twentieth century Debrecen conserved a very different character. In the eighteenth century it was almost impossible to draw a borderline between a village and a city in Hungary; there was no middle class and most city dwellers lived on agriculture. Though Debrecen was a trade center on the routes between North and South, East and West, and was also an important market town, its habitants belonged to that typical category of peasant-burghers, a social class unknown in Western Europe. Among its population there was also a growing number of intellectuals: doctors, lawyers, teachers, ministers, civil servants; their number amounted to about 450–500, of which 378 were so-called "togati" (students wearing a special gown), graduate students of the College of Debrecen.[9]

It is of great significance that, unlike the Northern cities and unlike the many newly emerging ones in which, encouraged by the Habsburgs, various ethnic groups settled after the Turkish occupation, Debrecen was a purely Hungarian community, where only Magyar was spoken. This proved a great asset to a poet who was to assume the role of creating a national culture. Csokonai duly acknowledged this fact in a letter when he hoped to be given the editorship of a Magyar magazine: "My abilities in the Hungarian language have been greatly increased by my having been born in Debrecen and by my spending twenty-two years of my youth there" (II, 865). The Calvinistic character of Csokonai's native city was no less help in his development, for Protestants, an underprivileged minority, were more representative of enlightened ideas. The citizens of Debrecen welcomed Emperor Joseph's reforms because they hoped to profit from religious tolerance. Indeed, Csokonai's father was an enthusiastic supporter of Josephinism for this reason. Also, through religious channels, through links with Protestant churches and faculties of theology in Germany, Holland, and Scotland, Debrecen was more open to ideas from the West than most Hungarian communities. The Calvinistic tradition promoted a certain democracy in city government, unmatched elsewhere in contemporary Hungary. Also, though austere, sober-minded, humorless Puritanism prevailed in the citizens' behavior patterns, their semipeasant stature helped to conserve a healthy, life-loving, down-to-earth instinct absent in truly urban communities.

During the Turkish occupation the size of the city had rapidly increased; harrassed villagers fled to Debrecen where they enjoyed greater protection. Trying to accommodate Turkish demands and to keep the Habsburgs away without giving up their own life-style, taught the city authorities the techniques of survival. Their many dangers contributed to making the citizens suspicious, inward looking, and short-sighted; these qualities do not endear them to outsiders. The twentieth-century poet, Árpád Tóth (a native like Csokonai of Debrecen) compared the city to a prison in "Invokáció Csokonai Vitéz Mihályhoz" ("An Invocation to Mihály Vitéz Csokonai"). Csokonai, said Tóth, once also "looked at Debrecen's tree bars, / as the prisoner looks at the jail bars." This strange image illustrates Debrecen's paradoxical nature; the city generates extreme love and extreme hatred. Many of its native sons, intellectuals, have experienced this love-hate relationship. When he compared Debrecen to a jail, Árpád Tóth had in mind the short-sighted stupidity of the Debrecen atmosphere, but as part of the city's paradoxical nature, this jail had pleasant features too, as indicated by the strange reference to trees. Tóth's reference is by no means accidental: the city's most attractive feature—now being destroyed by its present leadership—are its gardens. The famous "Nagyerdő" (Great Forest) and the many little gardens attached to small private houses, made Csokonai's Debrecen unique. This was the Debrecen he loved. The surprising attraction for a son of this rough, coarse, boorish city to rococo gardens becomes less strange if we read the poet's praise of Debrecen's garden-loving womanfolk of good taste who "can nurture nature's mild pomps so meekly" (II, 219).

As mentioned earlier, the city is both attractive and repulsive: it opens up doors into the wide world but then it destroys those who benefit from the openness. It destroys them since it vehemently resists everything new; it is slow in pace and unimaginative. Slowness alone can be a killer to quick minds; no wonder Csokonai bitterly complained: "everything progresses here on crabfeet" (II, 947). There is no better example of the fate of the intellectual in Debrecen than our poet's misfortunes: not only was he exiled in his lifetime, but he fared no better after his death, for in 1835 a campaign for collecting money to erect a new tombstone failed. The present century has not yet made amends. Csokonai's tomb has not been given attention. Quite recently the poet's admirers could still enjoy the view of the evening sunset in Csokonai's Darabos Street very much as he had centuries before. In the 1970s the city leadership destroyed the little streets around the college, full of historical and literary memories as well as charming old houses. Csokonai's statue, once the pride of the college-district, stands today in front of an ugly, cold office building, alien to the poet's spirit.

Ferencz Kazinczy, the Dr. Johnson and literary dictator of Csokonai's time, was absolutely right in his judgment of the dealings of the Debrecen city authorities: "their small-town mentality plays a frightening game." [10] He had every reason to be angry. Not only did Debrecen exile Csokonai but its authorities later provoked a controversy over the inscription for his tombstone. The city fathers asked Kazinczy for advice about a suitable text. With the sphere of artistic beauty in mind, he suggested: "I, too, lived in Arcadia." Since the term was unfamiliar to the peasant-burghers, they checked the unknown word in a dictionary and found that Arcadia was a place where

"there are good pastures for oxen and even better ones for asses."
Indignant over what they interpreted as Kazinczy's reference to
Debrecen, the citizens started the famous "Arcadia suit" which made
Debrecen the laughing stuff of the sophisticated.[11]

This strange story is literally true, and yet it demonstrates only a
half-truth about Debrecen. It cannot be and should not be ignored
that without Debrecen, which ultimately rejected him, Csokonai
would never have become the learned poet he was. If, on the one
hand, the Debrecen of Csokonai's days stood for the peasant bagpipe
as well as the "fokos" (a specific walking stick associated with folklife),
and for a slow, conservative sensibility, it also offered unique possibi-
lities for a young man who wanted to dedicate his life to the lute. Thus
we have already mentioned the charming gardens. Debrecen also
enjoyed the earliest communal musical culture in Hungary: a choir at
its college. The city also boasted an enlightened bishop, Sámuel
Szilágyi, who not only translated Voltaire's *Henriade*, the glorification of a tolerant ruler, but in the preface to the work made a liberal,
enlightened statement, unusual for a clergyman in Hungary at that
time. As he put it, "the writer of the book had to present the abuses of
religion by the superstitious and by those (fanatics) who pretend to
have witnessed appearances of God." [12] Among other enlightened
figures there was Lajos Domokos, a promoter of learning in the
vernacular and of secular power over church power in the manage-
ment of city affairs. There were also István Weszprémy, the learned
doctor trained in England, and quite a few other outstanding minds in
natural sciences, especially botany and medicine. The forward looking, enlightened attitude of the members of the so-called "Debrecen-
circle" (János Földi, Mihály Fazekas, Sámuel Diószegi, all friends of
Csokonai and Diószegi a relative) had a great impact on the poet's
development. In this group they read the French Encyclopedists,
cultivated gardens, welcomed Rousseau, and wrote serious botanical
works. The mastermind of the circle, Földi, of half-noble, half-
plebeian background, son of an impoverished gentleman turned
craftsman, was a translator, a doctor, an expert on versification, a true
polyhistor like most members of the group; no wonder Csokonai
became one himself. Among these friends young Csokonai found a
unique thought-nourishing environment in the very midst of boorish,
austere, conservative Debrecen.

As for their political attitude, the members of that circle were
progressive, enlightened sages supporting progress but opposed to
violence, bloodshed, and war. Debrecen also gave the country the

first editor of a newspaper in Magyar, Sándor Szacsvay, an enthusiastic supporter of the French Revolution when it began, and as far as
censorship permitted. He did not condone excesses of violence
either. On August 3, 1791, his *Magyar Kurir (Hungarian Courier)*
published a fictive letter by Henry IV of France in which the late king
chastized the French, who though they "wanted to give an example to
the whole world in enlightened good morals, in the improvement of
learning and craftsmanship," mistreated their king.[13]

It is an open question how far the Martinovics conspiracy was a
factor in Csokonai's expulsion from the College of Debrecen if,
indeed, it was a factor. We cannot be sure of the true reasons. The
college, two hundred years old at that time, was an integral part of
Debrecen as is now the university, reflecting its very paradoxical
spirit. The college minutes speak of frequent misbehavior: Csokonai's
permissive attitudes with his students, his unorthodox method of
taking them to the Great Forest for teaching, his unsavory dispute
with one of the professors who originally got him the job of teaching
assistant, but who later provoked the poet's pride and was allegedly
ridiculed by him in front of students for his affair with a servant-girl
whom he got pregnant. There was also the problem of Csokonai's
failure to account properly for some money he had collected for the
college on a preaching tour, and his unaccounted for prolonged
absence at this time.[14] It was during this absence that he visited Pest
(the capital of Hungary was Pest at that time with Buda being a
separate settlement) right at the time when the executions of the
members of the Martinovics conspiracy took place there in 1795. The
authorities may have been overcautious. Debrecen, the most rebellious Hungarian city, where in 1849 Kossuth dethroned the Habsburgs, has frequently been the most cautious city as well, zealously
eager to obey the wishes of, and to show allegiance to, any authority,
probably a sad legacy of Turkish times. We know that the city was
hard put to it to prove its innocence against renewed allegations of
involvement in rebellious activities. The Magyar text of the "Marseil-
laise" as well as three hundred copies of Martinovics's most outspoken anonymous letter to the emperor of Austria had allegedly
been sent to the city for circulation. We also know that Gerzson
Fodor, a former student of the college and a teacher of Csokonai,
was tried for allegedly participating in the conspiracy, and that László
Szabó Szentjóbi, another student of the college, was actually sen-
tenced to prison. Caution, then, was well grounded. "The hard-
headed, stubborn, *stutzig* and clumsy citizens of Debrecen were

intolerant against every one who was not of their religion or nationality." [15] What is important is the intolerance against everything different, and Csokonai, a genius, was most certainly different. The exact reason for his expulsion from the college does not really matter; what matters is that many a great writer of the nation grew up at the College of Debrecen and none of them was appreciated there. All of them had unhappy or at least mixed memories about their Debrecen years. The most touching and truthful book about this college which played the role of a British Oxford and Cambridge in the history of Hungarian literature, is found in Zsigmond Móricz's *Légy jó mindhalálig (Be Faithful unto Death)*, a novel about a little peasant boy who could not have received an education anywhere else in Hungary but at the College of Debrecen, but who at the same time was made utterly miserable by that college and by that city.

IV *The College of Debrecen and Csokonai*

The Englishman Townson described that famous institution in 1793 in these terms: "the building is irregular, old, and decaying. Yet often in such dismal abodes not only deep learning has been acquired but genius has been taught to shine in words of fancy." [16] Little did he know how well his words applied to a young man who was a student there at the time of his visit. With 3,000 students the college was a giant institution in Hungarian terms, educating teachers and ministers for almost the entire country, but most specifically for the area east of the river Tisza. The college established almost one hundred secondary schools in the country and over one hundred primary schools worked under Debrecen-trained teachers. Ever since its founding in the sixteenth century during the Reformation, the college maintained a close relationship with the Scottish Presbyterian Church and with Protestant churches in Holland and Germany. The students sent abroad for study were instructed to bring back books as token of their gratitude; in this way, the college acquired a remarkable library. The college was also a school in democracy, with a system of student self-government: the younger boys, the so-called "servant students," had to perform all kinds of chores for the "togati." The student body was socially mixed, and included sons of both the gentry and the peasantry. Some of the latter had free meals with city families. Though the difference between "servant students" and "togati" was enormous, they all formed a unique democratic community. They came from all over the country bringing their specific regional experiences and thus enlarging everybody's knowledge about the country as a whole. They also received elementary, secondary, as well as higher education at this unique institution. With the library, this treasure fund of knowledge, and the learned professors on the one hand, and with the often unruly student body on the other, the college offered two extremes to Csokonai and he drew heavily on both. The standards of the college were rigid, representing the inflexible, gloomy, austere, Puritanical ethic, but, with its emphasis on moral seriousness and responsibility, it promoted a commitment to community that prepared Csokonai for his lifelong dedication to knowledge and to the national good. The very strict system of behavior and discipline that controlled life at the college hampered Csokonai's love for liberty and independence. On the other hand, the library offered a wonderful opportunity for his curious mind, and understanding professors like József Háló Kovács, the Hungarian translator of *The Aeneid*, eased the regulations for this outstanding student.

When Csokonai entered the college that institution already had a glorious tradition of exceptional professors. Indeed, the eighteenth century was its heyday with professors qualified to serve at Western universities, for example, István Hatvany, the physicist, who declined invitations to various posts abroad preferring to serve his native city, and György Maróthy who had introduced the polyphonic singing that had provided the basis for Csokonai's musical training. The students formed all sorts of study groups; the most famous were the copperplate engravers. Close friends of the poet, they took care of the dying Csokonai. The first Hungarian map of the North American continent was their work under the guidance of the learned Ézsaiás Budai, who, too, had taught the poet. Before Csokonai, Ádám Horváth Pálóczi, a poet himself, studied there and was expelled. This college then, like the city, was Janus-faced. On the one hand, it acted as a kindler of the flames of curiosity, but unfortunately, also as an extinguisher of those flames. And the line never ended. At Csokonai's funeral among the mourning students there was Ferenc Kölcsey, the author of the Hungarian national anthem, then fifteen.

CHAPTER 2

The Making of the Poet

I Background

CRITICS have emphasized differing aspects of Csokonai's multi-faceted poetry. In consequence, his name has become associated with the peak of Hungarian classicism, with the best in rococo, but also with preromanticism and the emergence of folk lyric so fashionable in the nineteenth century. Such a variety should not surprise us, for the arts in Western Europe of the eighteenth century were eclectic, with works of utterly different formal features standing side by side, as Arnold Hauser has pointed out in his discussion of architecture, painting, and poetry.[1] Csokonai is unique as a single artist combining in his own poetry elements of the rococo, the classicism and the sentimentalism of his own time with the baroque and the mannerism of an earlier period; he transcended them in the direction of the romantic, and an even more modern lyric. Most of his great poems are not easy to classify, since he integrated in them the best of all styles at a high level of maturity. Among his works we find minor masterpieces in almost every style, and others combining several styles in one single, sometimes very short poem. Csokonai's eclecticism is rooted in his eagerness to absorb the totality of the European culture of his time and to create through perfect absorption a unique Hungarian equivalent. No period of his career can be associated with a single style. While classicism for philosophical topics, and rococo as well as mannerism for love poetry dominated his early Debrecen years, none of these styles entirely disappeared later. Enriched by sentimental and romantic elements—which better suited his increasingly frustrated mood—all those styles lost their conventional features as they developed into a mature poet's personal way of expression.

His poetic career started when he was eleven. In his development

27

he relied basically on three sources. First, there was the traditional poetical training at the College of Debrecen, mostly classical. The students were required to practice versification in two main types of poems: descriptions of given objects, seasons of nature, or types of persons, and arguments for moral issues. The young Csokonai soon gained the attention and appreciation of his teachers. His so-called *Zsengék (Juvenilia)* (partly in Hungarian, partly in Latin) became the basis of his later great philosophical poems; already in 1794 he was praised in the *Magyar Hírmondó (Hungarian News)*. There he announced the forthcoming publication of his works in four volumes including mostly translations but also originals like *Békaegérharc (The Battle of the Frogs and the Mice)*, the drama *Tempefői*, many songs with notes, and numerous essays. The ambitious plan never materialized; unfortunate events in the life of the poet and the nation intervened.

Csokonai's second source of inspiration was Vienna, the source of most cultural news for Hungary at that time. It was not always the best and the greatest whose fame reached him through Austrian channels in distant Debrecen.[2] Indeed, he was superior to many of his models. He relied on two then popular reference books, Eschenburg's and Johann Georg Sulzer's. His range of knowledge was amazing, and included, besides the ancients, the English poets Milton, James Hervey, Pope; the French Voltaire, Rousseau, Diderot, Holbach; the Germans Gessner, Bürger, Kotzebue, Ewald Kleist, Schikaneder, Blumauer, and most possibly Herder; and from the Italian Tasso, Ariosto, Guarini, Metastasio, to mention only those who obviously influenced his own writing. The impact of the Italians seems overwhelming. As a student he participated in a study group in which each member pledged himself to learn a language and to study and then present to the others the literature in that language. They also subscribed to periodicals paid for out of their own money. Csokonai chose Italian. We have no definite information that would explain his choice and we are limited to guesses. Two possible reasons should be considered; probably a combination of the two prompted his decision. At the end of the eighteenth century, Vienna was dominated by Italian culture, with Metastasio the most admired poet. Also to be considered is the young poet's early interest in the musical effect of poetry. Indeed, though his *Juvenilia* were far from perfection, writing them provided a splendid exercise for the future master of Hungarian verse; actually they form the basis of Csokonai's amazing versatility; almost a child, in those school exercises he cre-

> Become the angelic *butterfly*,
> In Olympian gardens,
>
> Where from one life
> To another with wings
> It drinks eternal youth
> From roses grown in the *spheres*?

The poet seems to be asking for death, but death realized in terms of the birth of the butterfly is something else. When death means becoming butterfly, it means cheerfulness, beauty, and eternal life in the Olympian gardens of poetry; indeed, this is an ideal world of escape, good therapy for the poet's perturbed spirits.

III   *The Rococo Csokonai*

Csokonai's rococo aspect can be best defined in the words Arnold Hauser used in attributing Watteau's greatness to "the expression of both the promise and the inadequacy of life, to the always present feeling of an inexpressible loss and an unattainable goal, to the knowledge of a lost homeland and the Utopian remoteness of real happiness." [4] Hungarian Marxists are trying to build up a radical, democratic image of Csokonai and are embarrassed by the seeming incongruity between Csokonai's adherence to the rococo and the illuminated ideas he propagated in some of his poetry.[5] A close look at the contemporary European scene reveals that neoclassical Pope had his rococo moments and enlightened Voltaire rejoiced in rococo poignancy and coquettry. There is an increasing tendency in contemporary scholarship to accept the *rococo* as the dominant style of the eighteenth century and to recognize the fact that the ideas of the Enlightenment were frequently expressed in a rococo manner.[6]

In his book on the essence of the rococo, Helmut Hatzfield underlined the wider implications of a reference by a Marivaux character to "instruction through amusement." [7] Indeed, instruction through amusement was Csokonai's lifelong endeavor. In his early career at the College of Debrecen, he was, in modern terms, "the poet in residence," and also a kind of "coterie poet" catering for the small circle of students. Later he tried to enlarge his appeal by aiming at the whole nation. Since one of his main goals was to elevate the Magyar language and to educate the taste of the public, rococo refinement seemed the most appropriate method. He set himself a task similar to that of Addison and Steele with *The Tatler* and *The Spectator*. For beauty he tried the baroque too, but the rococo, less violent, more gentle, and more subdued, proved a better guide to good taste. Informative in this respect are two prose documents: his farewell address to the students at the college before his expulsion in 1795 and his letter to Koháry in 1797.

In the farewell speech, delivered in Hungarian to the anger of the faculty, Csokonai presented his Muses as bearing "wreaths of roses of innocent pleasures." Poetry—he said—accompanied him "with a sweet ringing lute" whenever he was in a cheerful mood. "When I was sad"—he continued—"it opened its bosom of Ambrosia so that I could unburden my sorrows; there I let my tears run; it kissed them off my cheeks with comforting laments and I fancied myself in another world" (II, 796). In this confession the young poet gives an unambiguously rococo definition of his own poetry. The letter to Count Koháry explained the reason for his preference for this style, and the reason corresponds, indeed, to what Marivaux's character called "instruction through amusement." Because of the infant stage of Hungarian literature, Csokonai believed, it had to be handled with the same care and affection we would give a baby. "Sweet speech, alluring graciousness, singing, dolls and sugared dessert should be used to win it over to school training. It cannot even feel its own disease; consequently, if we want to give it medication, the rim of the bottle should be honeyed, the healing pills should be wrapped in raisins" (II, 824). In a word, Csokonai wanted to "sugarcoat the pill."

Certain rococo features stayed with the poet all his life in prose and in verse alike; in his early love poetry, though, they were dominant. Nightingales, turtledoves, roses, violets, scents, ambrosia, the dallying with love, the cult of mirth, charm, sighs, kisses, pastoral pleasantness, a preference for ambiguous erotic situations, the delight in the miniature, tears, dew, groves, brooks, the riot of scents, colors, and tastes, the lover's wish to spy on his nymph undressing, a carefree, coquettish atmosphere, a sensuous, voluptuous, erotic tone, all these are part of the early love poems which Csokonai—then a student in Debrecen—wrote probably to two different girls or to no specific person. With their grace and charm, these poems prove that artificiality can be attractive. Though their dominant tone is mirth, to call them bittersweet would be more correct. As in Mozart's lovely rococo music, so in Csokonai's poems we feel the vibration of sadness and hidden frustration under the stylized mask.

The second stanza of "Víg élet a Parnasszuson" ("The Good Life on the Parnassus") sounds almost like an enumeration of the most important rococo features:

> Here the Muses themselves are the leaders.
> They let you taste their nectar.
> Apollo himself will sing now and then;
> Echo will answer from time to time.
> Here you can hear cheerful music, sounds
> Of Aganippe trickling among sweet shrubs.

Pleasant sights, tastes, scents, and sounds are all represented here. The Hungarian system of verbs is superbly adequate to render this miniature world: the verbs, suggesting movements on a tiny, gracious scale, perfectly match the nouns, describing tiny sized objects or persons.

The poem "Keserédes" ("Bittersweet") is illustrative of the fashionable in the rococo sweetness in pain, what the Italians called *dolce picante*:

> The rose is a fair flower,
> Yet has sharp thorns.
> The bee gives honey
> but gives a poisoned sting.
> Rich wines lighten our spirits,
> then dull our senses.

In later years Csokonai returned to the same idea and refined it in "Édes keserűség" ("Sweet Bitterness"), a poem in four-line anapestic stanzas with beautifully rhyming couplets. The difference between the two poems indicates the increasing emphasis on the personal:

> I anguish, I pine away.
> I give myself up to grief;
> I stare at the ceiling till dawn,
> pitiful in my plight.

The last stanza reads like a declaration in verse of the merits of sweet bitterness:

> Ah, bitterness and honey!
> Delight and pain!
> With Cypria's sweet yoke,
> heavy on my neck!

"A patyolat" ("The Snow-White Voile") is one of Csokonai's first poems in the spying mode. The voile, preventing the lover from seeing his sweet-heart undressed, is called "little silk fog" and "tiny cloud." "A feredés" ("Bathing") reiterates the topic of spying. The turning from long lines to extremely short ones underlines the lover's impatience and conveys nervous urgency as he watches the water devouring the adored body. The water covering the maiden's body is sensuously described and in the end, a jealous poet expresses his envy of the happy waters that are allowed to make love to her. This poem is as close to mannerism as to rococo:

> Her ankles,
> her knees,
> her thighs—
> already her thighs
> pawed by hungry waves.
> You lecherous waves, draw back!
> If you go farther up,
> I shall defend her honor.
> Ah, you have killed me!
> You, her lovers.

The personification of the water augments the tone of sensuousness.

"Az elragadtatott érzékenységek" ("The Raptured Senses") is based on a kind of competition. The senses are trying to find out which one is responsible for the lady's exquisite beauty. "One little breeze" gently breathes "Ambrosia scent"; the body is rich in "beautiful colors"; "ivory shoulder," "rose lips," "snow-white bosom," "marble neck" all contribute to her beauty. "Deep sighs" and "faint voice" produce the sound effect. Not even "the rose's dew" is "frailer" than her limbs, and, of course, her "lips (are) sweeter than honey."

Though also an early poem, "Laura még ingó kegyelmed" ("Laura, Your Still Hesitating Mercy") displays features disgressing from the traditional rococo; the tone is more personal, and folkloric elements are mixed with the conventional devices. In stanza 5, the poet sings in easygoing, playful terms about the maiden's unfaithfulness, but in the last stanza the tone of deep-felt personal grief becomes unmistakable:

> Rather than conjure the right word
> to curse you,
> I pity you, while deep down
> I pardon you, sweet pearl.

"Sweet pearl," literally "pearl shape"—emphasizing the graceful beauty as well as the pricelessness of the beloved—is among the most beautiful terms in Csokonai's lyric, and in Hungarian poetry for that matter; it is a word he coined and caused much controversy among critics. The frustrated lover is not angry; he is forgiving. Indeed, forgiveness will be characteristic of Csokonai's great love poetry.

To use the poet's own term, "Egy tulipánthoz" ("To a Tulip"), later revised as "Tartózkodó szérelem" ("Shy Request") is a true rococo pearl, full of grace, charm, tenderness, easy playfulness, music, dedicated to the cult of flowers, with an ambiguous mixture of mirth and grief. An early poem, it is the poet's masterpiece in the rococo style:

> Mighty love's
> devouring fire hurts me;
> you are physician to my wounds,
> bright, little tulip.
>
> Your sure eyes shine
> like dawn's great fire:
> your lips' dew—
> ointment for my lesions.
>
> Accomplish with comforting words
> what this lover asks,
> and with a thousand kisses worthy of gods
> I will pay your fee.

In its superb simiplicity, the poem comes close to folksongs where the flower motif is as important as in the pastoral. Those critics who vehemently object to Csokonai's rococo style fail to realize the close connection between Csokonai's pastoral and his poems in the folk-art manner.

"A muzsikáló szépség" ("The Beauty Making Music") is one of the very few later love poems entirely in the rococo vein. The poem is about Lilla playing her instrument and about the effect of her song on the poet-lover. He speaks about the girl's appearance in terms of "melting" and "heaven's full happiness." When she starts singing and playing, the poet's ears and eyes become totally confused by the lovely riot of voices and flowers which, combined, exercise an over-whelming charm; the poet's soul is "defeated," his ears and eyes enchanted, confused:

> Sounds are flowers

on your singing lips;
flowers are sounds
from your delicate fingers.

IV   *Mannerism and Csokonai*

A close look at the poet's best in this style reveals affinities with the
English Metaphysicals.[8] Mario Praz's characterization of Crashaw
has a striking validity for Csokonai: "His faith belongs to the kind
which finds an outlet in expressions now sour and eager with longing,
now instinct with melting sweetness."[9] And hardly could a better
statement be found about Csokonai's art than T. S. Eliot's judgment
on Marvell: "this alliance of levity and seriousness."[10] It is, of course,
not easy to draw the dividing line between rococo and mannerism in
continental European art. The two styles mingle so closely in Csokonai's poetry that they are almost inseparable. The most we can say is
that in the rococo, in spite of a certain touch of decadence, the
dominant mode is easy pleasantness, while frivolity, poignancy, and
virtuosity convey a kind of tension in mannerism. Mannerism is a
highly intellectual art in which deliberateness is of the greatest
importance. Deliberate asymmetry, deliberate distortion of reality,
deliberate playing out of an assumed role, deliberate creation of
confusion form the basis of the main device of that style: the use of
fantastic, striking, witty conceits. Dr. Johnson, with his classical
standards, found that those conceits were "violently yoking together
incongruous elements"; the very same conceits struck the romantic
Coleridge as "the balance and reconciliation of opposites." For Csokonai, this master of eclecticism, the conceit meant classical balance
achieved through artistically applied asymmetry. In his mature art, it
became a device for creating balance between the real and the
dreamworld. The blurring of the borderline between life and death in
some of his great poems is a manifestation of that "world of mingled
reality" which in Arnold Hauser's view is what mannerism is all
about.[11] Our modern sense of relativity and our readiness to accept
opposing truths pervades this style. The feeling of insecurity, of a lack
of stability, constitutes the background of mannerism, "the artistic
expression of crisis," as Hauser calls it.[12] Csokonai lived in an age of
crisis. His country was in a critical situation; his own life was crisis-
ridden, an ocean of misery and degradation; in consequence, this
mode of expression appealed to him.
Another characteristic of mannerism also played an important role

in Csokonai's artistic development: the tendency to replace classical normativity by a more subjective approach.[13] It is this feature which makes his best poetry so surprisingly modern, a fact that reminds the reader that Metaphysical poetry was one of the major shaping forces in T. S. Eliot's art. Though at his best Csokonai transcended the artificiality of mannerism, the ambivalent relationship between nature and art never entirely disappeared from his poetry. Art does not imitate nature, it creates like nature,[14] as Hauser said of mannerism. This thought leads to a modern conception of art as the innumerable "isms" at the turn of this century interpreted it. The goal "épater le bourgeois," stupefy the bourgeois, seems almost identical with the ideals of the Italian mannerist, Marino, in whose view the poet's aim is to create wonder, shock, and amazement.

There are almost no poems by Csokonai where mannerism is evident in its pure form without mingling with other styles. An early poem, from the *Juvenilia*, "Barátságos búcsúvétel" ("A Friendly Farewell") uses geographical metaphors recalling Marvell's

> Thou by the Indian Ganges' side
> Shouldst rubies find, I by the tides
> Of Humber would complain.

Csokonai asserts that physical apartness will not separate two true lovers, and he places himself in imagination "on Spitzberg's snowy peaks" and his maiden on some tropical shore among painted savages, but even though—he says—"would my evening your morning be, / I would still live and die with you."

The conceit in the early poem "A dél" ("The Noon") is based on the irreconcilable opposition between heat and cold, fire and water. The artificial twist of making the lady's coldness responsible for the fire in the poet's heart, meets to perfection J. S. Smith's requirement of a model conceit whose elements "can enter solid union and at the same time maintain their warring identity." [15] One of Csokonai's best-known descriptive poems, "A dél" starts with a realistic picture of a typical scene on the great Hungarian plainland in Debrecen's vicinity, when the sun is high. The picture of the sun rising to its peak, the languid air, with nature almost at boiling point, the cattle withdrawing to the shade of a beechtree to rest and ruminate, remind native readers of some of the most beautiful passages of the nineteenth-century poet János Arany, and thus carry special significance. The poem goes on describing birds, bees, lizards, grasshoppers, and tired travelers. Suddenly the descriptive style turns into something different. The heat reminds the poet of his passion, and the poem switches to the lover's burning with the heat of love. The paradox is stretched to its wildest extreme and fulfills Marino's demand that the poet must shock. Referring to the pain caused by love's flames, Csokonai comes to the crucial question: his suffering has been caused by the maiden's icy coldness, by unreturned love: he is burning with love and yet his heart is cold; in the end, the lover is moved to tears. This striking performance of Amor's is compared to Jupiter's activity as he fires his lightnings in the rain.

Of a different character, almost classical in its balanced beauty, is the lovely, charming poem "Földi Rózsa" ("Rose Földi"), written to the wife of his friend, János Földi. There is no convincing evidence to sustain some critics' suggestion of a love affair between Csokonai and Mrs. Földi, not even of a student's admiring love for a married woman; it simply may be a situation or role played out. In the poem Csokonai addresses a rose that could have blossomed in one of Debrecen's many gardens. He is tempted to pick it, but then has second thoughts; the rose is best left to flourish to maturity in the garden where it belongs:

> Open, lovely and smiling
> rosebud, open now.
> Open. Wandering in the dawn,
> mild breezes wait to kiss you.
>
> Bloom, tender flower
> Hebe draws nectar, gives you that blush;
> Flora, drapes your neck
> with a velvet robe.
>
> Oh, you will adorn
> this tiny garden;
> Oh, how much we want to pluck
> that rose from you.

The poet resists temptation; the rosebud stays on and will live and give birth to a baby rose. And suddenly the poem turns into a prophecy about a baby daughter to Rose Földi; a uniquely lovely confusion is created; the poet is talking about the flower rose baby and Rose's baby Rose at the same time. The charming playfulness of the sustained conceit rests on puns. Rose is a female name and at the same time the name of a flower. Földi is the last name of Rose's husband, and the literal meaning of the word in Hungarian is "of earth." This permits the poet to tell that the Rose, both flower and child, was "nurtured by earth's moisture." At the end of the poem, Csokonai sees himself as a forty year old middle-aged man talking to the now blooming young Rose about the prophecy, while the girl, "flowering with rose colors" will kiss the poet's "icy hands."

A later poem in the style of mannerism, "A hévség" ("The Heat") is based on the paradoxical similarity between the heat devouring the poet and the heat devastating nature. "Canicule burns, / parching the green field" begins the description of drooping, languidly fainting nature. The second stanza, however, is entirely personal:

> In me, too, a fire.
> They say it's Cupid,
> I don't know who—
> Not his name anyway—
> Enough that he burns in my bosom
> devours my soul with his intensity.
> I am drying up,
> Can hardly catch my breath.

Nothing is left of the artificial tone but the slight mythological reference to Cupid. In the best Metaphysical vein, Csokonai turns to everyday, conversational language which then continues into the third stanza by picturing the refreshing, reviving effect of relief bringing rain:

> Yesterday there came soft
> drops, a little rain
> soaking forest
> and field with new life.
> And look, the drying flowers
> revived with the first drops,
> the tree's curled leaves,
> opened green again.

A shorter last stanza contains the poet's most personal reflections and wishes, without interrupting the continuity of the original conceit.

> Oh, if only on me,
> On my fainting head,

such life-giving water
would drop and slack my thirst.

V   *Csokonai and Folklore*

In the view of the twentieth-century writer and critic, László
Németh, with Csokonai the folk itself entered into Hungarian poetry.[16] The roots of the poet's interest in folk art can be traced to two
sources. One is the philosophy of the Enlightenment: the teaching
about natural people generated a search into the hitherto neglected
treasure fund of popular literatures all over Europe. Also, at the
College of Debrecen, peasant boys mixed with sons of higher classes
in the student body: from their native villages they brought their
regional songs with them and thus enriched the college's collection of
folksongs. In the confused and divided state of the country, the
development of the vernacular was a main issue, and Csokonai believed in the regenerating influence of the idiom of the common folk.
He reminded fellow writers: "Men of letters! do not read only foreign
writers, but seek out the simple working Hungarian in his forests, on
his Scythian plains, search for the third-rate songbooks, the provoca-
tive sermons, the vulgar romances spread out on the shepherd's felt
cloak, listen carefully to the singing lassies and the simple lads" (II,
214).

Moreover, there is no doubt that Csokonai's beloved rococo also
has affinities with the folklore, at least in the use of flower imagery,
and the elements of the two are often so successfully fused that some
critics would range a love poem with folksongs, while others would
label the same a rococo pastoral. Rousseau's "back to nature" initiated
a wave of criticism against the artificiality of the pastoral, and yet, the
shepherd of that same pastoral was indirectly responsible for the
emergence of the peasant in Hungarian poetry, though, at first, in a
highly stylized way. The so-called *Victoria* songbook, from the
second half of the eighteenth century, in its chapter "Notae Hungar-
iae Variae" ("Various Hungarian Notes") includes quite a few rococo
songs with a folksy touch calling them "flower songs for the drawing-
room," for example: "White swan in tears, / my heart whirls in
burning fire." [17] Tears, burning fire, and swan belong to the inven-
tory of refined poetry. On the other hand, these opening lines reflect
the lover's emotional state, and thus use a common device of folk
poetry. In folksongs nature's sympathy with man is often emphasized
by nature's identical mood with that of the speaker. In a more subtle

way and sometimes on a more sophisticated scale, this combination frequently occurs in Csokonai's poetry as well.

Recently Hungarian critics have paid increased attention to the remarkable kinship between Csokonai and Robert Burns.[18] In the eighteenth century, Scotland was dominated by England as Hungary was by Austria. Also, because of its support for the Pretender, Scotland was in a confused political situation. Both countries prided themselves on a glorious past, and in both poets were trying to write in the vernacular. Burns and Csokonai represent a kind of synthesis in the cultural development of their respective nations; they stand for the peak of the Enlightenment in their individual countries; they also have close links with folklore and at the same time are indebted to the rococo. In many of Burns' popular poems the Scottish lad sounds like a pastoral cavalier. In its playfulness, "The Lass that made the Bed" displays all rococo qualities of sensuality:

> Her bosom was the drive snaw
>   Twa drifted heaps sae fair to see;
> Her limbs the polish'd marble stane,
>   The lass that made the bed to me.[19]

Such poems alternate with others clearly popular though in a pastoral setting, like

> The sky was blue, the wind was still,
>   The moon was shining clearly;
> I set her down, wi' right good will,
>   Among the rigs o'barley:
> I kent her heart was a' my ain;
>   I love'd her most sincerely;
> I kiss'd her owre and owre again,
>   Among the rigs o' barley.[20]

Both Burns and Csokonai collected popular songs. In its search for knowledge, the Enlightenment led to the discovery of the culture of diverse small nations, and it also led to the strengthening of national consciousness among them. Burns and Csokonai are outstanding representatives of this new trend, of the emergence of small nations on the scene of world literature. This led to the disruption of the uniform cultural pattern of eighteenth-century Europe. While most Western-European nations presented the ideals of the Enlightenment in the same way, Scotland and the newly emerging Eastern-

European nations burst on the cultural scene with a fresh, daringly
new, forward-pointing, courageous combination of conflicting styles.
All these literatures drew heavily on the powerful heritage of the
common people. Independently of each other, Burns and Csokonai
were part of the same development.

In Csokonai's "Parasztdal" ("Peasant Song"), of the type known as a
"situation song," the swain sings in simple words to his Kató who has
been locked in by her wicked stepmother. Though written in iambic
feet, the rhythm of the poem is unmistakably that of Hungarian
folksongs. The structural arrangement also follows the folksong pattern and the image of nature associated with the lover's basic feeling
emphasizes the emotional tension:

> A quiet evening,
> without a breeze.
> and yet? look a shivering
> aspen leaf.
> Oh, my fair Kató! not as much shivering
> in that leaf
> as in me for you.

The sixth stanza returns to the evening scene. The lad notices the
smoke rising from the hut. The smoke reminds him of love's fire in his
heart and leads to more laments. He decides to rescue Kató, but
surprised by night's darkness, the lover leaves on a reiterated note of
lament.

One of Csokonai's best-known poems is "Szerelemdal a csikósbőrös
kulacshoz" ("Love-Song to the Wooden Canteen Covered with Pony
Skin"). It is less obviously folksonglike than the above discussed
"Peasant Song." The skillful, witty adoption of Ewald Kleist's motif in
his "Liebeslied an die Weinflasche" ("Love-Song to the Wine-
Bottle") to a Hungarian peasant situation is reminiscent of mannerism. The use of the sustained conceit, an intellectual game, diminishes the simplicity so important to the folksong, yet does so without
ultimately damaging the poem's freshness and spontaneity. As in
many similar poems, Csokonai used the so-called "old Hungarian
eight syllable" form, and with his virtuous handling he creates a
special effect. In its confusion of styles, the poem is a good example of
Csokonai's eclecticism, with elements of folksong and mannerism, of
rococo piquantry, of features of the wine song, and attached to all this,
of the ambiguity of the death wish. The poem opens with a jovial
declaration of love to the canteen:

> Dear treasure, ootsume-wootsume,
> pony-skinned canteen
> for you I die, for you I live.
> I wouldn't trade you for a hundred lusty wenches.

The poem then continues with a praise of the "body" of the loved one, as "On your slim waist the shoulders / are straight without the whalebone corset— / not like Mimie's / or you know whose." Later, the erotic images multiply as the conceit is carried out to its fullest, and the poet goes to bed with his "lover":

> How often we slept together
> (and not even married)
> Tonight again, if I doze,
> We'll sleep together, won't we my love?

If we think the analogy has been stretched too far, we are mistaken. Wit has its ways, and so the fantasy goes on:

> Oh, if only from such consummation of our love,
> little flasks were born
> and would sit in a neat row
> on the shelf, full of wine!
>
> If only for my wife
> I could trade you in
> so that you could give me such sons and daughters
> sweet canteen.

However, the mood suddenly changes. The poet feels death's closeness. In an unexpected switch, instead of the marriage bed, Csokonai makes us face a burial feast:

> Oh, I kiss you and hold you
> as long I breathe.
> And then, we will be buried together
> under this inscription. . . .

And here once more we return to the teasing, playful tone:

> "Traveler, toast with pint of wine
> this simple, resting soul of mine
> and his helpmate in all done and seen,
> his faithful pony-skinned canteen."

The pony-skinned canteen was a necessary ingredient of any Hungarian shepherd's equipment, and, in the region of Debrecen is still available for practical use on excursions and as a tourist souvenir.

Another of the poet's folksongs that was sung all over the country in the nineteenth century together with genuine ones is "Szegény Zsuzsi a táborozáskor" ("Poor Susie at the Time of the Enlistment"). It is a situation song: a lass laments over her lover's leaving and joining the army ready for war. The poem has come down to us in two different versions which many critics regard as evidence of a hesitating attitude. It is significant, though, that the earlier version contains both the last stanza reminiscent of the manner of the aristocratic love lyric, with the lady encouraging the warrior to return victorious from battle, and a preceding one which, more than any other part of the poem, sounds like a genuine folksong:

> Black earth, evil path.
> There my lover rides toward death,
> a cap on his head,
> the sun in his eyes.

The identification with nature, characteristic in popular verse, comes through perfectly; the black earth and the evil path correspond to the gloomy farewell of the peasant-lovers. The fact that Csokonai dropped both these stanzas from the later version invalidates the conclusion that the omission of the aristocratic-sounding last stanza marks a democratic shift in Csokonai's attitude.[21] Along with folksonglike elements rococo features are not lacking in this poem either:

> Weeping, I went to his quarters—
> From there to the garden's end.
> My tongue began my sad song
> like the song of the lone dove.

The dove and the garden are reminiscent of the rococo. The grief, however, is neither artificial nor decadent; on the contrary, it strikes us genuine and highly justified:

> At the trumpet's call,
> He mounted his horse, rushed
> off to fight the Turk—
> probably for ever.

The novelist Zsigmond Móricz preferred the masculine and yet gentle "Megkövetés" ("An Apology") with rhythm and beat in a truly popular vein.[22] There is a love game involved in this mature poem, but unlike the ambiguous flirtation in rococo poems, everything is genuine, simple, and forthright in "An Apology":

> If you are angry, I am sorry;
> Let us, love, be reconciled.
> I only said, "*I love you*,"
> Was that the word that angered you?

The poem's ending matches the initial playfulness of the love game, and yet the natural simplicity and purity of tone are preserved all through.

> If so, I'm sorry,
> give that sweet word back, Lilla.
> I won't be angry for it.
> For that word I can forgive a hundred times.

"Habozás" ("Hesitation") is a dialogue in twelve-syllable lines, each in three beats, the common rhythm of Hungarian folksongs. No less reminiscent of genuine folksongs is the theme itself: farewell. Also the lover's playful delaying his departure is a frequent device in Hungarian folksongs. "Were I able, I would leave town. / But Lilla loves me. / I could easily put grey streets behind / If she would go with me." Consecutive stanzas offer variations on the condition game, like "Laughing I would pack my lute in my wagon / If she, with me, rode high behind the team." Lilla intervenes only after the condition is changed into an unconditional resolution of not leaving. After receiving the maiden's pledge of love, the poet agrees to go but not without reassuring her of his feelings. The two join in a duo: "Don't worry: this heart beats for you." Dialogues, little enacted dramas, are, of course, an extension of monologue-situation songs. Robert Burns used them too. No better proof of the success of Csokonai's excursion into folk poetry than his songs' popularity among the people, and the popularity of the poet himself, who, soon after his death, became the central figure of stories and anecdotes about wandering students.

VI   *Vulgarism and Naturalism in Csokonai's Poetry*

Often critics find it an embarrassment that some of Csokonai's best poems and many of his minor masterpieces display disturbing signs of churlishness. As already pointed out, our poet, with his remarkable flexibility, represented the totality of his age in all its complexity. A touch of the vulgar belonged as much to the rococo as to the poet's native environment. The rococo was by no means homogeneous, and besides Marivaux's refined and pleasant "badinage" it also accommodated Diderot's sometimes all too outspoken obscenity. Mannerism, too, has two sides. English Cavalier poetry mixed pleasant elegance with spiciness. Nor was such a mixture alien to Burns, who at least collaborated in some bawdy songs. As for some of Csokonai's immediate models, the German Bürger enjoyed student obscenity and the Austrian Blumauer became famous for the vulgar. The poet's native environment acted as a reinforcing agent. The very fashionable, congratulatory "name-day" poetry (in Hungary, a person's saint's day rather than his birthday would be celebrated) was oriented to an all-male audience and was marked by vulgar lewdness; of course, the students, too, delighted in coarse and sensual verse. The most obvious example for this style is a rather long poem, "A pendelbergi vár formája s megvétele" ("The Form and Siege of the Castle of Pendelberg"), based on the conceit that the woman is a castle to be taken by a siege of males. Intellectual cleverness, wit, the delight of thinking up all possible variations on all possible parts of the female body are carried to the extreme, and there is scarcely a line without some lascivious ribaldry! Even among the poet's other bawdy pieces this one is unparalleled in indecency, and on top of everything it is written in classical twelve-syllable couplets. The physiological description goes into lengthy details that does not miss any kind of physical function, sound, or smell of the body. The student audience is remembered at the end when somebody calls "Pendelbergia" not so much a fortress as a college offering more knowledge than most schools. It is suggested that the castle should be kept open for the benefit of youth. Csokonai was well aware that such details could displease the censor as much as radical ideas. No wonder he reassured Count Széchenyi that as far as serious ideas were concerned, he would avoid "everything that in the present situation could be shocking," and as to the pleasant field, he would avoid "all obscenity and prank" (II, 899).

The poet did not spare himself either. In one of his early poems he applied the disrespectful, earthly speech of students to describe his own unattractive outward appearance. In "Rút ábrázat és szép ész" ("Hideous Face and Fair Soul"), Csokonai addresses a friend: "You say, my friend, that I am hideous, / and my face's abominations are great." Then follows the detailed description of the face as that of a "scaring crow," resembling a "hideous fuzz-ball" grown "on horse's excrement." However, Csokonai does not spare the fair-faced friend either, and repays unpleasant comments in kind, comparing the wonderful white face to "the goat's buttocks."

Csokonai acquired excellence in observing details when writing his descriptive poems as school exercises. This practice as well as the rococo's interest in minute details, paved the way to the poet's naturalistic, down-to-earth approach in later mature poems. In consequence, artificial rococo had qualities which helped the development of the poet to a style fundamentally opposed to rococo elegance. The great literary dictator in Hungary at that time, Ferenc Kazinczy, disliked this down-to-earth, realistic tendency in Csokonai's art and considered it a menace to the refinement of taste; indeed, he bitterly complained in a letter to a friend: "He was among our writers like the painters of the Netherland school, and I have worked continuously against this school; I have pointed out that we should not paint according to nature but should always emphasize the Beautiful, the Ideal." [23] Fortunately, Csokonai, though he respected Kazinczy, went his own way. Ultimately, he transcended the rococo and mannerism; transcended the vulgar also, but not before he had absorbed its useful ingredients, such as an outspokenness about the unpleasant, seamy sides of life. Without this reverence for details, pleasant and repellent, a poem like his last one, the iambic "Tüdő-gyúladásomról" ("On My Pneumonia") would never have been written. Here, physical and mental sufferings come alive with naturalistic details. In his presentation of sickness, of the life of the sick man, the poet makes use of as various styles as the rococo and the sentimental. The bed becomes a coffin and then again a boat floating with the sick poet on "the dark waves" of "dubious hope and sure fear" and of life and death:

> Ascendant Moon! behold my torment.
> What is this I lie on—
> is it a restless bed,

> or is it a coffin?
> No, It is a boat which on dubious
> hopes and sure fears—
> life's and death's dark
> waves—is adrift with me.

The gentle zephyr of the rococo turns into a sirocco parching the
lungs, and the crypts of sentimental poetry send out an icy wind.
Thus, the real ague shaking the ailing poet is suggested by images of
obviously artificial poetry. Similarly, the arrow of love mythology,
standing behind his heart, suggests the menace of death, while "two
deaths kick with their heels" on "the stone wall of the breast." The
conceit of the poet's swinging on the waves is continued as he rocks to
different shores. Various sights greet him; they come from various
styles of his poetry and range from romantic "bare caves" to gracious
rococo gardens. The metaphors of ice and heat used with so much
skill in earlier artificial poems with sophisticated deliberateness,
become frightening and real:

> I choke, I breathe: I freeze, I burn.
> One or the other kills me.
> I faint, feel, revive—
> a horrible death or life.

And then a most welcome change as the poet's feverish mind mistakes
the visiting doctor for "golden recovery," a kind of heavenly vision. It
comes lavishly accompanied by ingredients of gracious poetry and
touches the ailing body with "rose fingers." The poet immediately
feels ready to return to his "tiny lute":

> You touched with rose fingers
> my breast's dark vault
> and with your eyes, sparked
> life's pulse.
> Already, my soul, like phoenix,
> rising from the flames.
> And at my trembling fingers,
> my tiny lute sings once more.

And then a twist once more. From the borderline between death and
life the poet returns to life. In the last stanza Csokonai regains
consciousness and recognizes in the white specter his doctor and

friend. Enjoying a temporary relief from physical pain, he sings in thankfulness to his friend:

> It is my Sándorffy who keeps vigil—to this
> I owe what life is left?
> Ring, resound, silent evening!
> Gratitude makes me sing.
> I owe a double sacred duty:
> to the doctor and the friend.

He was grateful and expressed thankfulness as he best could, in poetry. However, this clearing of the hallucinating mind may well have been the very last, the one immediately preceding death!

VII   *The Baroque,*[24] *the Romantic, and the Modern Csokonai*

Arnold Hauser's reflections and explanations about the emergence of modern art and its stages as it developed from mannerism through the romantics to our age, are a most useful guide in the assessment of Csokonai's poetry. A genius, born in the right environment, at the right time, when everything was ready for an unbalancing and upsetting of normative principles in poetry, our poet seems to have illustrated in his *oeuvre* in a unique way the development of the European artistic mentality through the centuries. Hauser describes the development prepared by the Renaissance as "the subjectivization of the artistic world-view." [25] Formerly, artists attempted to imitate nature, a world they believed they knew and the knowledge about which was commonly shared by all since it was supposedly objective. The new approach, as it slowly developed, took an entirely different stand; now the important thing was not to know the laws of nature; what mattered was experience. The objective, normative view was abandoned; the goal of art as imitation was replaced by the endeavor to express the artist's subjective impressions of reality. The real breakthrough came with the romantic attitude, as Hauser explains, that substituted self-experience for the experience of the world and that regarded the world as the raw material of personal experience, more real than external reality.[26] The artist gave up the normative objectivity of classicism; as a unique individual he—from now on—presented his private view of the world. From a public figure, a kind of spokesman for commonly shared ideas of universal interest, he became a private person expressing his inner world, or the external world as he experienced and envisaged it.

At first glance it appears that Csokonai was destined to be the former type. In the beginning of his career he enjoyed the encouragement of a sympathetic and understanding student audience, and then as well as later in his career many of his poems were generated by occasions of social or public interest. Moreover, the link between public affairs and literature was particularly strong all over Eastern Europe, where the assertion of a national cultural identity accompanied or preceded national independence. Csokonai was nurtured on the ideals of the Age of Reason with an emphasis on the power of knowledge and the importance of commonly shared values. Nonetheless, by nature he was a most private person, prone to subjectivity: a romantic conception of poetry was close to his heart. He made it perfectly clear in his preface to his occasional poetry that he disliked writing those poems. Like the romantics, he considered inspiration the true source of art. He did not call it inspiration, though, but used the Latin term *vena* instead. "Not even the greatest poet has it in his power to command *vena* "—he said—"though he were asked to write for the name day of the Chinese emperor. *Vena* has an irresistable power and sometimes it gets you into such a passionate state that you have to give up food, sweet sleep and visiting with good friends" (II, 228). *Vena* then is, in Csokonai's view, responsible for starting the creative process, while in the classical view the poet does not really need it. With adequate craftsmanship he will always be able to render the objective, unchanging outside world according to the normative rules of art. However, if the poet is to express his private view of the world, inspiration becomes indispensable. And indeed, as time went by, and the hope of becoming recognized as the public voice of his nation dwindled away, Csokonai more and more made poetry the vehicle of personal confessions.

Such a reorientation, then, toward greater emphasis on his own inner vision and on his own experiences of life and of reality, came to the poet because of unhappy circumstances in his life that turned him after his exile from the college into an uprooted wanderer, "a professional guest" [27] in friendly homes, but without a home of his own. Overwhelmed by deep personal grief, by the loss of his native environment, and by the loss of the girl he loved, he abandoned playfulness. The artificial dreamworld, which he formerly had deliberately ornated in the rococo style, turned into a personal dreamworld where he escaped from the real. Dim, flickering, and diffuse lights replaced the bright clearness of the former imagery as Csokonai turned with Ossianic nostalgia from the present to the past. Alienation too, a characteristic of the modern artist who feels cut off from common humanity, became a personal experience. His ode "A magánossághoz" ("To Solitude") treats the theme of loneliness in the most personal terms; in consequence, the poem is unlike the classical ode which excels in the universal treatment of this subject matter. There are some ingredients of sentimental poetry in this ode as in many other mature poems, but Csokonai transcends the conventional practice of this manner with the simplicity of his complaint. Though he incorporated elements of the prevailing sentimental trend by now he was well on his way to finding his own personal mode of expression; thus, those of his poems that display preromantic traits, unlike his early rococo poems, cannot be easily associated with a style.

On the other hand, his youth and early death link him with the Romantic Age, a period of literature hallmarked by poets who all died young: Shelley, Keats, Pushkin, Lermontov, Musset, etc. The disruption of the classical balance and proportion in Csokonai's poems written after his expulsion from the college, the turbulent, somber, and sometimes paradoxical images, a passionate, visionary character in his poems on war or Hungarian history, clearly indicate a closeness to the romantic attitude.

At the sime time, those very visionary elements have baroque overtones as well. The bizarre, extravagant, confused nature of the baroque corresponded to the poet's lack of stability, the baroque's lack of clarity to this own state of mind. Originally a violent reaction to the new Copernican world view, the baroque is one of the many styles paving the way to the modern.[28] There is no better indication of this than the modernization of the baroque vision in Csokonai's art.[29] His "Az 1741-diki Diéta" ("The 1741 Diet") displays conventional, mostly theatrical baroque elements. In this poem of disproportionately complex structure, Hungarian history is presented in a prophetic vision. Theatricality and all other conventions disappear in later mature poems when visions become emotional, personal, filled with existentialist shudder of the infinite, the unmeasurable, the unknowable, the uncertainties of the human condition. His poem "Újesztendei gondolatok" ("New Year Thoughts") is full of visions like

> Perhaps because of you, oh time,
> you who destroys everything we have and are,
> even the sun is burning to coal.

Though his last philosophical poem, "Halotti versek" ("Funeral Poems"), written shortly before his death, recapitulates on a higher

level the ideas of his earlier enlightened poetry, classical discipline
and proportion are altogether lacking. And above all, gone is the firm
belief in the problem-solving capacity of human reason. Rationality
no longer seems to be the answer, or at least not the only answer. The
poet turns to revelation as strongly as to philosophy—thus admitting
with the romantics that logic may not be the only way. Indeed,
instead of the rational presentation of ideas we are struck in this poem
by illogical visions and hallucinations worthy of the baroque but also
of the romantics, and with anguish close to that of the existentialists.
It is the modern, alienated individual in despair with his expressionis-
tic nightmares whose voice we hear, not that of the enlightened poet:

> God, my Creator: If I must dissipate to nothing,
> how much of it is your work?
> Even *hope*, my chief physician,
> is only your false gift, yours, Executioner, Murderer.

Not only is his concern with the common fate of mankind—death—
expressed in agonizing private terms, but personal suffering and pain
also disrupt the quiet, calm, serene tone of his earlier poetry and
burst into tormented outcries like in "Az utolsó szerencsétlenség"
("The Last Misfortune"):

> From marrow-drying fires,
> my head hums wedged and heavy
> because my feelings go rank.
> My heart beats, I choke.
> I can do nothing
> but feel and suffer.
> My soul and body are sick to death.
> Heaven, earth, my treasure, forgive!

CHAPTER 3

The Essayist and the Creator of Genres

I Csokonai: the Poet of the Nation

THE eighteenth century attributed to the poet a public role as
spokesman and propagator of the ideas of the Enlightenment.
Writers assumed various functions as scholars, philosophers, journal-
ists, and politicians. But in Hungary all this was almost impossible in
Csokonai's lifetime: publication was not easy; there were few journalistic opportunities, and after the 1795 Martinovics trials any public
role with ideological connotations became an impossibility. On the
other hand, because of the political dependence on Austria, literature
and language were soon recognized as political issues. As the nation
slowly matured into a literary audience, it learned to accept literature
as its moral and political guide. Csokonai, however, had to break the
ground. It is by no means accidental that the beginnings of the
missionary role of the Hungarian poet go back to the eighteenth
century. The philosophy of the Enlightenment was conducive to an
atmosphere in which such a commitment could emerge. The Enlightenment believed in the power of the written word. The ideology-
shaping activity of a Voltaire and a Rousseau convinced Hungarian
writers of their own responsibilities in shaping the national consciousness, if their writings reached an audience at all. One significant
aspect of Csokonai's career was his desperate fight and losing battle to
achieve publicity. He never really saw the publication of any of his
important original works. With his verse-journal, A Diétai Magyar
Múzsa (The Diet's Hugarian Muse) he made an attempt to create for
himself a public among the nobility assembled for the duration of the
diet, and later he tried three times to enter a journalistic career. In
1798 in Komárom he hoped to gain the support of Count Széchenyi
for the continuation of one of the first periodicals in Magyar, Min-
denes Gyűjtemény (Collections of All Kinds) whose publication came
to a halt with the death of its first editor. In the letter asking for

patronage, he made his reasons very clear: "let us accustom the public to reading, let us tame the Asiatic moral, let us refine the Hungarian taste" (II, 832). In 1801 he was planning to launch a newspaper in Magyar in Pest. In the same year he had a slight and short-lived hope of becoming the editor of a Hungarian paper issued in Vienna. All these plans were frustrated as were his hopes for seeing his works published.

In spite of these and many more failures, Csokonai never gave up. His own conception of the poet's role in the nation's life has come down to us in various prose writings. The first treatise giving insight into his cultural policy, "A magyar nyelv feléledése" ("The Awakening of the Magyar Language"), was written around 1790, at a time when political controversy centered on the language issue. The enlightened Emperor Joseph decreed that German should replace the outdated Latin, and the nation united to insure that the vernacular gained recognition. Csokonai called Latin "a rusty key to knowledge" and considered its continued use in education an obstacle in the way of cultural progress. He also pointed out that German, not unlike Hungarian in his days, had once been in much need of refinement. The second part of the essay is a prose poem in praise of the Magyar tongue.

Magyar language! the language of my dear nation! I first started to speak in you, the sweet name mother first reached my ear in you, you made the air that I first breathed in tremble around my cradle, you filled the air with the kind words of my teachers, of my compatriots, of those who loved me; through you my infant mouth first asked for Hungarian food; in your fragmented parts the first ideas of my infant brain started to burst into the open like the tiny beams of the emerging dawn when it becomes light. All through the changing fortunes of my youthful days, the common talk of life and the sweet talk of friendship rang sweet to me in you. Through you my mind's thoughts continuously rose higher than in any other language and I found more pleasure in writings in your pleasant pen than in the most scholarly works by foreigners. Satisfied and amid a thousand delights swang my youthful Muse on your musical terms like a new born butterfly among flowers and tulips. (II, 127)

The flower and garden terminology in this context strongly underlines the fact that to Csokonai it meant more than a conventional literary device, for he often turned to this vocabulary to express sincere and even sacred feelings.

Very soon after some of the participants of the Martinovics conspiracy had been executed and others imprisoned, voicing political purposes even in the cultural field became unwise. No wonder that the expelled young teaching assistant never dispatched his letter to Count Koháry, in which, in 1797, he provided a comprehensive account of the cultural scene. A few years later, Csokonai rewrote it in a slightly different version addressed to Count Széchenyi. The letter opens with a survey of the fortunes and misfortunes of Hungarian literature, referring to the brief period of hope before the Martinovics conspiracy was disclosed, a hope "that knowledge which is at home among refined nations will discover us here in Europe's eastern part." In agreement with the light and dark imagery of the Enlightenment, this passage ends with a statement about the present situation: "We fell back into night." Next follows a passage of lament about the decay of everything Hungarian because of the continuous misfortunes that had accompanied the nation ever since they had left the Asiatic homeland. Perceptive Csokonai measured the distance between his native land and Western Europe in "centuries," carefully examining all signs of backwardness: the state of the vernacular, that of the national theater buried in its infant stage, the lack of printing presses operated by Hungarians, the indifference to reading. In consequence of all this, the poet concludes in dismay: "Our whole nation lingers behind in deadly dumbness." The passage that follows is a frightening prophecy of the death of the nation without any kindred in Europe, a vision that has been hunting Hungarians throughout their history. Csokonai could see only one way to prevent this from happening: Hungarians must apply their legendary bravery this time not on the battlefield but to the cultural challenge of overtaking the West.

Next comes the poet's famous description of Magyar literature in the infant stage, and the proposal to cure it with the sweetness of poetry. Csokonai illustrates his point by Italian, English, and German examples and notices that Petrarch preceded Galileo, Chaucer preceded Newton, and Opitz preceded Kant. He himself promised to serve the nation with philosophical and other scholarly works at a later stage, but for the moment he offered his poetry, "the tiny tender shoots of spring in a little garden," as the most adequate gift to his country. In order to be in a position to serve the nation, to reach people, the poet needed the count's financial assistance so that he could publish, "to help his Muse to existence"—as he put it (II, 822–27). It is important to understand that while the publication of his works was significant to him on the personal level, the public and personal goals were so closely linked that the dividing line is almost nonexistent.

Csokonai was serious about scholarly activity and was well qualified to comment on it. This superknowledgeable poet's interest was not restricted to the humanities; he was willing to study geometry and to acquire a knowledge of geodesy in order to get a job. His friendship with Földi, Diószegi, and Fazekas may be responsible for his extended knowledge in the field of botany. Such expertise encouraged him to seek work in the Georgikon, the agricultural college founded by Count Festetich. He even volunteered to undertake a study trip to Switzerland to obtain firsthand knowledge of dairy farming. That was in 1798. In 1803 he proposed to translate Linnaeus' work into Hungarian. As a true poet of the Enlightenment, he wrote a poem on an encyclopedia and crowded his poetry with all sorts of scholarly information, thus turning it into a compendium of information. As László Németh most perceptively remarked, "encyclopedias are hidden in his poems."[1] His notes, e.g., to his mock-epic *Dorottya*, cover mythology, literature, botany, zoology, geography, lexicography, etc. He also planned to edit the works of his friend Földi, those of the seventeenth-century poet Miklós Zrinyi, and he provided entries for a planned dictionary.

At the end of his life he desperately tried to get a job as a librarian in the newly founded National Library. He wrote to the generous donor, Count Széchenyi, but the response was negative, though Csokonai was perfectly qualified, and he could have used the books for his historical background research for the national epic *Árpád*. We have little exact information of how knowledgeable he was in the visual arts; in one of his essays he mentions "the claire-obscure" of painting (II, 222). His familiarity with music is a well-established fact; he even started a "Muzsikális gyűjtemények" ("Musical Collections") in several issues, and was planning to write the text to music (II, 973). Besides this we have the musical inserts in his dramas. He had the making of a literary critic, as is demonstrated by his only attempt in that field, the detailed criticism of Gábor Dayka's poems.

Csokonai was also an excellent translator; his wide-ranging activity in this field from the ancients to the moderns, from poetry to philosophical essays fitted perfectly into his cultural program, partly as an opener of windows into knowledge and partly as a means of refining the language. In his preface to the translation of Ewald Kleist's "Frűhling," Csokonai made a point of emphasizing that he engaged in such activity only as public service (II, 236). What he really enjoyed, according to the preface to *Dorottya*, was creative writing. As he said, he would have preferred to be an average original poet to being a first-rate translator (I, 479). However, as a duty to the nation he spared neither energy, knowledge, nor inventiveness in this performance. He considered the enrichment of the vocabulary as one of the main duties of an efficient translator, since the original Magyar vocabulary could hardly satisfy eighteenth-century needs. Csokonai wanted the language to develop in various ways: by reviving dialect and archaic words as well as by utilizing assimiliated ones from other languages. He considered the various means as parts of the natural growth of the language. He himself "pushed new branches according the nature of the language" (II, 240), as he so beautifully expressed it in gardening terms.

Teaching was another field compatible with the enlightened poet's image. Csokonai fulfilled this important function on two occasions. From the accounts of his students we know something about his performance as the teacher of the poetry class at the College of Debrecen. They gave us evidence of Csokonai's dedication, of his sensitivity to their needs, of their informal relationship, of the unorthodox method of walking with them in the city's famous Nagyerdő (Great Forest). The inspiration of Rousseau's *Émile* is obvious, but it is equally true that his own disposition took him in the same direction. More direct confirmation is found in the letters about his teaching in Csurgó. They reveal that he wrote textbooks for his (approximately) nine students. We cannot but admire the energy, sacrifice, and concern for these almost illiterate peasant boys for whom Csokonai tried to provide an education on the highest level of the age. He wanted the books "with the best principles and the best system" (II, 842). Strongly opposed to the old-fashioned method of memorizing, he intended to replace it by teaching his pupils to think. No wonder, the students had only the best of memories of this dedicated teacher for whom punishment was unnecessary.

II *Csokonai's Theoretical Activity*

Dedication and commitment to serve the common good in the field of culture made Csokonai the first theoritician in literature in Hungary. His broad perspective is as surprising as the many-sidedness of his creative work. It is amazing to see this homeless, jobless, "professional guest" dreaming up in backward Hungary the vision of a Hungarian Writers' Association that would convene a gathering of European poets. Only recently has the Latin plan been found for an international Helicon, a publication of that organization.[2] Csokonai envisaged a chapter on aesthetics, both historical and theoretical, with a kind of *Gesamtkunstwerk* in mind, since he proposed to deal with supplementary fields like music and painting. The chapter on poetry is well outlined in the sketch; the issues he proposed for discussion are strikingly modern: like the nature of the poet's genius, the service of poetry to mankind. With an early understanding for the sociology of literature, he listed among the topics to be discussed the reasons for the bloom and the decay of literature at certain ages among certain nations. He also planned a debate about the relative value of the moderns and the ancients, a much argued question in the poet's own time. In line with the Schlegelian idea he suggested a discussion on national literatures from the Orientals (Chinese, Indian, Arabic, Persian, Turkish, and Hungarian) to the Westerners (ancient Greek, Latin, Spanish, Italian, French, English, Celtic, and Czech). In the best scholarly tradition, he also provided for detailed philological notes. One wonders how he could space himself for so many things!

The plan, of course, was unrealistic. Given the political situation, no Hungarian Writers' Association was a possibility in Csokonai's lifetime, nor could such an organization have convened an international gathering. The plan is nonetheless important because it displays the insight of an exceptional mind into all major theoretical problems of world literature at a time when such an idea was not yet recognized or understood. In backward Hungary, cut off from the direct intercourse and flow of ideas, Csokonai foresaw a deepening interest in national literatures, and he did not limit himself to Europe; the Asiatic origin of the Magyar nation may have been an important factor in the poet's broad scope of interest. He also looked to more organized collaboration between writers in different languages, and a closer relationship among the various arts. He anticipated the concerns of the romantics with genius, but also the concern of the later nineteenth century with issues such as time and environment and their effect on literature. Only a person actively engaged in theoretical problems could have dreamed up such an amazing plan.

Most of his essays are about literary genres. In the eighteenth century, classification by genres dominated literary scholarship, and Csokonai followed this custom. His concern for genres explains his eagerness to create in Magyar literary forms not yet represented in the language.

The essay "Az epopeáról közönségesen" ("On the Epic in General") gives a definition of the genre, points out the importance of the characters, of the plot, and of the manner of presentation for classifying the various types of epic. A historical survey includes Homer, Virgil, Tasso, Milton, Voltaire, Klopstock, Pope, Boileau, and Blumauer. The poet then proudly mentions his own works as the only examples in Hungarian of the mock-heroic. In distinguishing between different types—the heroic, the knightly, and the mock-epic, as well as between different protagonists—the hero and the knight, Csokonai touches on the modern problem of the nonheroic, average central character. The preface to his mock-epic *Dorottya* is a specific discussion of that genre. It also gives some insight into the poet's work. In a response to possible criticism that he might have ridiculed real personalities, Csokonai reveals the way his epic was written. In Csokonai's view the purpose of art has been achieved, "If with our lively and natural presentation we amaze the reader's, onlooker's, or listener's imagination so much that he is magically transferred from his real situation into our invented scene or passion as if that were a new world" (I, 472). However, beyond amazing the reader, the true poet also wishes to present "the goodness or evil, nobleness or weakness, wisdom or foolishness of the human heart" (I, 477). In Csokonai's understanding, then, literature has a message. As we have noted earlier, the didactic role of literature was consistent with both the ideas of the Enlightenment and the requirements of the Hungarian scene.

One of Csokonai's most significant essays is his treatise "A magyar prosodiáról" ("On Hungarian Prosody"). A great expert on all kinds of verse forms, musical Csokonai was virtually the creator of Hungarian verse. In his poetry he combined Hungarian, ancient Greek and Roman, as well as Western-European forms. He also discussed all three types in detail: the rhymed lines with alternating stressed and unstressed syllables, the unrhymed metric verse, and the combination of the metric form with rhyme. He gave rules as well as examples for varied and meaningful rhymes and rhythms. Because of the language barrier, however, the formal aspect of Csokonai's poetry had to be neglected in this monograph.

His essay "Az ázsiai poézisról" ("On Oriental Poetry"), a further proof of Csokonai's interest in world literature, also explains this special concern as part of the poet's search into the national background. It is a scholarly essay with full bibliographical annotation and references to books for further reading. His remarks on the radically different character of Oriental literatures and the difficulty for the Western mind to understand and to enjoy them, are perceptive and modern. Specific examples of Chinese, Indian, Turkish, Armenian, Persian, Arabic, and Tartar poetry testify to his knowledge in this field.

The essay "Jegyzések és értekezések az Anakreoni dalokra" ("Notes and Essays on the Anacreontic Songs") is the one best provided with bibliographical apparatus; it even has a dictionary attached and amazes the reader more than any other with the range of knowledge of this poet-scholar. The dictionary supplement served as an opportunity to enlarge on his language reforming principles. Some of the entries, like the one on "the wild strawberry," contain detailed botanical explanations as well as linguistic ones. There are historical references concerning the earlier use of the word in the language.

"Lilla, érzékeny dalok három könyvben" ("Lilla, Sentimental Songs in Three Books") is Csokonai's preface to the collection of his love poems. This is the most personal of the essays and explains in detail how his poetry developed, how strong personal emotions disrupted the composure of the public poet. Parts of the treatise read like a confession: "Very often as you can see in some of my poems, my imagination was involved with entirely different topics, and it recollected itself only when not resisting my heart's secret demands, Lilla's name has already sneaked into my verse" (II, 231–32). The poems included here are either in the rococo style or more frequently, strictly personal. In consequence, the term sentimental indicates rather an emphasis on, and involvement with, emotions than an adherence to the then fashionable style.

III   The Poet-Scholar and Folklore

That Csokonai was a learned poet should be clear by now. There is no contradiction in this poet-scholar's taking interest in folklore. Not only did the college environment push him in this direction, so did his studies. A vogue for collecting folksongs was starting to flood Europe. In 1799 in a list of his manuscripts Csokonai mentioned this item: "Ancient and recent Hungarian folksongs (Volkslieder [sic]) which following the example of other refined nations I have collected from manuscripts and orally in order to save them from oblivion. There are 300 to 400 of them" (II, 827). Though this collection has been lost, we know of Csokonai's continuous concern, for in a letter to Kazinczy he refers to his plan to write an essay on "Volkslieder," on their different character in different nations. He also planned a bibliography (II, 979).

Csokonai's interest in folklore was not limited to literature; some of his remarks are of ethnographic interest, like his description in *Dorottya* of the tricks used by outlaws to scatter sheep so that the shepherds would have a hard time to round them up. He even gives the geographical place, the Hortobágy, where such tricks were customary. Since this famous wide plainland is in the vicinity of Debrecen, he may have been writing from personal observation.

In another episode of the same mock-epic, a servant, named Gergő, relates the coarse tricks played by maids on the men servants. Csokonai felt that this scene may have offended the refined. As an excuse for this excursion into the vulgar he referred to the drama. Csokonai had Shakespeare in mind when he discussed the necessity of introducing episodes of low comedy for the benefit of the unsophisticated. Presumably, he was aiming at a nation-wide audience, something similar to the Elizabethan public combining the sophisticated and the groundlings. In the preface, Csokonai went out of his way to apologize to those preferring refinement; for them he provided a scene involving goddesses and nymphs following right after the servant episode (I, 477).

Csokonai was fascinated by folktales as well. The reaction of the characters to Szuszmir's tale in his early drama *Tempefői* makes Csokonai's own attitude ambivalent. He wrote the play at the age of twenty, still happy and sheltered by the college, fully enchanted by the promises of the Enlightenment, fully confident in the power of knowledge and suspicious of ignorance. In this drama the learned poet seems to collide with the poet who, besides agreeing with Voltaire, assimilated also Rousseau's admiration for the state of nature. *Tempefői* was written in 1793. The tale in question had been incorporated into a collection of folksongs at the college of Sárospatak in 1789; this must have been Csokonai's source. The tale, without any specific moral message, is about an excellent prince and his adventures. A very specific message, however, comes across in the ardent discussion between the two main female characters, two sisters. The heated argument centers around the theoretical question of the beautiful and the useful in art. According to Éva, who enjoys folktales, "beautiful is what pleases"; but Rozália maintains that art should inspire noble aspirations, should be useful, and that no such accomplishment can be expected from an ignorant peasant. In her judgment "their miserable tales are beautiful but have no value." Next, their argument shifts to the issue of the vernacular literature in the infant stage, in need of beautification; at this point Éva suggests that Rozália's beloved Hungarian books are ugly and in consequence, worthless. Rozália, on the other hand, vehemently defends them against the admirers of more refined foreign literatures (I, viii). The dispute is inconclusive; significantly, though, both sisters support Magyar art: Éva folklore, Rozália literature in the mother tongue. The inconclusiveness is symbolic. Young Csokonai seems not to have come to terms with himself about the issue. With his dedication to the spread of knowledge, he was confused and hesitant about the role of folklore in the development of his native literature. Folklore opened up new channels for the enrichment of both language and culture, but, at the same time, with its coarseness and boorishness it carried the menace of slowing down the process of refinement. Not unlike the political situation, the cultural one also was confused. In both fields the decision-making was harassing, and flexibility rather than dogmatic consistency was the wise stand. At a later stage Csokonai's hesitancy about the merits of folk art will disappear; he will come to realize that thoughts and impulses other than learned are by no means inferior.

IV Creating New Genres in Hungarian: Epic and Drama

A. The Epic

As part of his cultural mission, Csokonai created two new genres in Hungarian literature, the mock-epic and the drama.

His *Dorottya vagyis a Dámák diadala a Fársángon* (*Dorottya or the Ladies' Victory over Carnival*) has been given critical consideration as a satire on the nobility, as a great step forward in realism, and as a sign of the poet's desperate search for belonging.[3] All these implications have some validity; however, if we examine the epic in the context of the *oeuvre*, it becomes evident that *Dorottya* is the result of a deliberate, conscious creative act. In the preface as well as in the essay on the epic, Csokonai speaks with undisguised pride of having created the mock-heroic in Hungarian. "Whatever the merits of my creation"—he said—"nobody can deny that this is the first of its kind in the language" (II, 149). Not only is Belinda, the name of one of the ladies, indicative of Alexander Pope's influence, but Csokonai himself proudly conceded and emphasized the kinship with *The Rape of the Lock*, a work he himself may have translated.[4] It is obvious, then, that his ambition was to faithfully transplant to Hungarian soil a conventional genre. Thus there is no discrepancy, at least not in

Csokonai's conception, between his aim to satisfy the requirements of "verisimilitude," the creation of the illusion of the real, and the use of a *deus ex machina*. Such a device was a necessity in a work that had to equal Pope's, but it is an embarrassment to Marxist critics trying to present Csokonai's work as an example of impeccable realism. However, the divine machinery was indispensable to the learned poet, who could not afford to omit any of the epic features if he wanted to create a perfect example of the genre in Hungarian.

Similarly to *The Rape of the Lock*, in *Dorottya* the main source of the comic is the incongruity between the trivial subject matter and its treatment in the heroic epic manner. The trivial subject in *Dorottya* is the quarrel between an old maid, Dorottya and Prince Carnival, a quarrel that grows into an embittered battle. Disputes and rivalries between two contrasting figures belong to an old popular tradition, as do gibes at old maids. We do not know exactly where Csokonai found the idea and what made him choose the topic, but we know that *Dorottya* had some antecedents in his poetry. A look at them may have some relevance to the better understanding of the major work.

In the early poem "A tél" ("The Winter"), Carnival, personified, "jumps on the new snow not finding his place." Later he throws dinner parties, swings to cheerful music for dance, and sledges. Husband-hunting maidens, too, play a role in this early verse. "The Winter" belongs to descriptive poems, and in most of those school exercises the moral tone was preferable. The main theme, then, seems to be Csokonai's disapproval of reckless gaiety and revelling, to which he found superior the society of a Pope or a Gessner. Although in the mock-epic the poet does not participate in any of the celebrations, he is an acute observer. In the beginning he tries to join the ladies on the sledges, but they leave him behind. "They did not listen to me / and gave me no place on the sleds. / Exhausted, I jogged in their tracks." Mounted on the poet's help, Pegasus, he is reminded of a contemporary French achievement in ballooning: "I flew on the wings of Pegasus, / as did Mr. Blanchard who took to the air." Flying over the cheerful company, Csokonai looks into the sledges from above and sees everything, as Gil Blas did when he looked into people's homes from the roofs. The poet, an outsider to the easygoing stable world of partying ladies and lords, has the vantage point of the objective nonbelonger, thus creating a poetical document of culture-historical significance about customs, talk, and life-style of the nobility at the very end of the eighteenth century. All this goes well with his acknowledged purpose of "ridiculing the nation's luxury and

degradation and punishing the naughty and often mischievous sporting of the young" (I, 477). Csokonai hoped to improve that life-style
by exposing its emptiness, as Pope hoped to reconcile two families by
demonstrating to them the ridiculous triviality of the cause of their
dispute. Undoubtedly the English poet's aim was much less ambitious, and even that failed.

"A Fársáng búcsúzó szavai" ("Farewell Words of Carnival") is an
early anticlerical poem written in the heyday of Csokonai's commitment to the Enlightenment. He did not consider the mock-epic a
suitable genre for arguments about ideological issues. The third
poem to be discussed, "Dorottya kínjai" ("Dorottya's Pains"), a
dramatic monologue, suggests that Csokonai's basic approach may
have been a deep human understanding of another suffering human
being. Dorottya laments about the pains of unrequited love:

> When we danced, the Lord's hand
> was icy in mine
> and however passionately I squeezed,
> his hand gave nothing back.

The intriguing problem about Dorottya is how far she is truly ridiculous. How far does Csokonai delight in jeering at her, and when does
he want us to stop laughing and to see the real person, the genuine
suffering behind the ridiculous, because excessive, manifestations of
her frustrated search and longing for a husband. It is this desperate
search that leads into such exaggerated behavior; she is ridiculous
because she is different from the norm, which at a carnival ball is to be
young, beautiful, and cheerful. Dorottya is different, but significantly
so was frustrated, jobless, homeless Csokonai among those who tried
to shelter him in Western Hungary. We cannot help suspecting that
besides providing for all the necessary ingredients of the genre, the
poet probably unconsciously identified himself with Dorottya's hope-
less situation. Indeed, Dorottya's problem could have no solution in
the real world, and the divine intervention, the epic device, is
paradoxically the only "real" means by which Dorottya can be married happily in Hungary's Somogy County where the ball takes place;
similarly, only a "miracle" could have solved Csokonai's problems. In
the real world Dorottya could not become young and beautiful, nor
could Csokonai find a patron or a publisher. Csokonai must have
viewed ironically the truth that while Venus solved Dorottya's dilemma in the fictional world of the epic, no divine intervention gave a
happy twist to his own fate.

Dorottya begins with an invocation to a bottle of wine that will kindle the flame of fantasy in the Muse. Csokonai then dedicates his work to a lady. It is most unlikely that she will ever read it: "At least if you do not read my book, / you can use the pages with your curling iron." The epic is accompanied by a multitude of philological notes explaining details of mythology, geography, botany, vocabulary, etc. One note refers to the fact that before having been applied to the lady's hair, the curling iron was usually tried out on a piece of paper: "the misfortune of many a poor book of poetry" (I, 481). The clue to the affinity between the poet and Dorottya is that they are both despised in their environment: Dorottya because she is old and wrinkled, and Csokonai because he is poor and a poet.

The work itself consists of four books in twelve-syllable couplets covering events of twenty-four hours, thus adhering to the classical principle of unity of time. In the beginning of each book the poet gives a brief summary. Book 1 tells what happens before noon. The procession of sledges takes cavaliers and ladies to the place of entertainment. The fair ladies are introduced in the rococo manner; some are beautiful, e.g., Amália: "Her smiling lips were like the opening rose / and each kiss became sugar." Not so Dorottya; her age and ugliness come alive: "Old age powdered her hair / and broke all of her teeth except two." As all sit at the luncheon table, including Opor, the male hero, Carnival and Hymen arrive with the book of records where they check the names of the unmarried women. Dorottya and her peers are left utterly unhappy; their age group is not even considered. In a moment of sincere compassion, Carnival notices this grief: "Like lonely violets on the desert sand, / they cry alone over being alone." Here the violet of the rococo is coupled with the idea of loneliness emphasized by terms like "cry," "desert," "alone." Concerned that their grief may damage the cheerful atmosphere, Carnival orders music and dance to begin immediately. Occasionally, then, this genuinely comic writing comes very close to sadness. Comic and tragic seem to mix here as do sweet and bitter, life and death elsewhere in Csokonai's poetry. The poet's own feeling of frustration and loneliness bursts into the alien atmosphere of joy and partying.

Book 2 presents the activities until the evening. The description of various dances is its most famous passage. First come the gracious foreign dances, then suddenly one nobleman suggests a return to the Hungarian tradition. Grace is now replaced by dignity: "majestic stand," "manly faces," and "haughtiness." All who look at the cavaliers realize that "In them Asia's uppity haughtiness / decorates Europe's refined manner." These two lines sum up the maxims of

Csokonai's approach to cultural policy: not to give up the native heritage but to preserve it while embracing the cultural gifts of enlightened Europe. Once the dances are over games follow with pledges. Dorottya is mocked and she is ready to burst with anger. There is enough motivation, but the poet-scholar knows the rules of the game and dutifully introduces the *deus ex machina*. Here comes the god of discord, hidden in a soft doughnut, not too hard for Dorottya's teeth. Once she has swallowed him, she is ready for combat. Her famous monologue makes us laugh, but on second thought we almost pity her:

> Why did heaven make me a woman?
> or why did it create men?
> If I were not a woman or there were no men,
> my sweet happiness would not have turned sour.
> But alas, I am old and pining away,
> with time my pains grow greater.
> A dismal solitude dries up my life,
> and sends me unmarried to my grave.

As the desperate old maids gather around her they make an altar of a chamber pot, and outraged and furious they burn locks of hair, love letters, etc. with sulphur candles.

In book 3, the dance goes on until midnight. Fury overtakes Dorottya again as she is pining on her couch:

> And her soul fed on anger's meager poison;
> now it was possible to see
> that she could turn crimson.
> The redness soon vanished,
> turning to blue, from blue to yellow.
> Her mouth moved as if in speech,
> but nothing made sense in her rage.

The old women prepare to take revenge on the cavaliers. As the god of discord secretely replaces the Jew, who so far provided the dance music, disharmony fills the rooms, chaos takes over, and the battle begins. Amor, however, plays a trick on the ladies: "Many, very many, almost half-dead, / fell to the ground or into the cavaliers' laps," wounded of course, by Amor's arrow. Opor then strikes on a fabulous idea; he announces that he and his followers will each marry the damsel who kisses them first. All the women forget their anger and battle; they rush to be the happy first with Opor.

Book 4, telling the events to dawn, portrays the cavaliers' rallying around Opor and defending him from the ladies. Defeated, Dorottya prepares to die. She is writing her will when Rebecca, who captured Carnival, Hymen, and the ominous book, interrupts her. After the book has been burned, preparations are made for Carnival's execution. Somebody suddenly cries: fire, and Carnival escapes in the confusion.

There are two significant digressions in this last book. One is the male servant's account of mischievous practices of the servant-girls, an episode mentioned earlier; the other, a speech by the nymph Fama. She reveals that everybody is angry because of the shortness of the carnival season. Many people in different walks of life, most of them in the middle class, have severe financial losses; seamstresses, tailors, who can sell fewer costumes, joiners, who cannot sell so many cradles, gypsies, who are invited to fewer weddings to play music, even priests, who collect less in fees for wedding ceremonies. In these two episodes, Csokonai introduces non–nobles—in the person of the servant Gergő the peasantry directly, and in Fama's speech the craftsmen, who are affected by the life of the nobility in financial terms, indirectly.

After these digressions Csolonai returns to the furious Dorottya. Anger, however, will have no opportunity to cause more trouble. The final *deus ex machina* appears in the person of Cythera in a golden carriage and with all paraphernalia of the rococo: "On her milk-white lap her little son plays with arrows— / in his eyes, fire; on his lips, ambrosia." While Cythera promises a longer carnival season for the following year and immediate rejuvenation for everybody present, Amor successfully aims his arrows at the hearts of Opor and the now young and beautiful Dorottya. Before the epic is over, they get married.

What is significant about *Dorottya* is the newness of the genre in Hungarian. Csokonai was for the new, because only the new could bring about the much needed progress. Characteristic in this regard is his comment on new words in one of the notes to the mock-epic: "Who does not like new words, should give up new ideas as well" (I, 544). Indeed, the refreshing air of newness pervades this work in many ways in an attempt to sweep over the stagnating country.

Besides creating the mock-epic, Csokonai also hoped to produce a national epic. "I want to be the author of *Árpád*"—said Csokonai in his essay on the genre (II, 149). His letters from the last years of his life give an idea how seriously he took this wish and how much research he made into the origins of the nation: the theme of the planned work, to which he intended to dedicate the rest of his life. The neoclassical respect for Homer and Virgil explains why several eighteenth-century writers were hoping to do for the Hungarian nation what these ancient authors had performed for the Greeks and Romans. An increasing interest in, and appreciation of, the Hungarian past pervaded Csokonai's poetry after 1795 as his hope for meaningful changes in the near future diminished. The short fragment, *Árpád vagy a magyarok megtelepedése (Árpád or the Settlement of the Magyars)* belongs to a series of abortive attempts in Hungarian literature that in the early nineteenth century finally led to the birth of a romantic national epic. Csokonai's work was planned to consist of twelve books. The plan itself is the work of the poet of the Enlightenment in whose interest culture and the Muses dominate bloody historical events. In consequence, culture-oriented issues get too much attention for an epic dedicated to a nation's glorious past. Moreover, the plan is future-oriented. The Muses' request to sing in the vernacular will not be granted for nine hundred years, and only a happier tenth century will witness the fulfillment of their and the poet's hope.

All that Csokonai ever finished, or at least all that has survived, is a Virgil-like invocation to the Muses in hexameters. The work begins in a heavy baroque style but Csokonai's preferred rococo soon takes over. The main character Árpád, a national hero, is neither heroic, mighty, powerful, courageous, or valiant. This protagonist of a national epic is twice referred to as terrible ("terrible knight" and "terrible Árpád") as if Csokonai were not sure whether Árpád was one of the glorious heroes of the past, or one of the murderers "on the butcher's block" of history, as he described war-dominated Hungarian history in an early poem. He praises Árpád, though, for settling down the Magyars in their European home and giving them laws, a laudable performance in the eyes of a poet of the Enlightenment.

Csokonai soon gets tired of "the god of the Magyars" who led the nation in battles; he turns to "the gods of sweetness." These gods seem out of place in a heroic epic. Moreover, reverting from the sublime to the pleasant, Csokonai presents an overwhelming number of rococo images. Even terrible Árpád is given a wreath of roses. The soft breeze, scent of balsam and roses, the languishing nightingale's sweet moaning are as much out of place in a Virgilian epic as the gentle milk of fair taste or the Muse's sacred grove. This Muse languishly weeps in the moonlight over the memories of the past and behaves rather like the Muse of sentimental poetry than that of an heroic epic. "Be thy song sweet!" sounds a strange closing sentence for an invocation to an epic about a terrible hero. This discrepancy between Csokonai's inclination for the "sweet" and this "terrible" hero, terrible perhaps because he looked at him from under roses in the moonlight, makes us believe that *Árpád*, had Csokonai ever finished it, would have been a hybrid genre, a work about a national hero and bloody events softened with sweetness and rococo diction. The poet must have been aware of this disharmony. The many love scenes he was planning to introduce would have provided adequate excuse for the "gods of sweetness" to take over and dominate the poem.

B. The Dramas

Csokonai was a lyricist. Not only his epic but his dramas too were a digression from his main inclination. Also, very much like his epic, dramas were written in active response to the needs of the cultural scene. There was no Hungarian drama of any literary merit in Csokonai's time nor was there any permanent Hungarian theater. When, in 1793, the twenty-year-old Csokonai offered sixteen comedies to the recently established Magyar theater in Pest, he was carried away by youthful, patriotic enthusiasm into an impossible suggestion. However, what is truly remarkable here is not the number, but the fact that this student who had no firsthand knowledge of a real theater, who had probably never seen a worthwhile theatrical performance in all his life, this student of the college in that most puritanical of all Hungarian cities, Debrecen, whose attitudes were unfriendly to the idea of the theater, had the courage and the imagination to attempt a response to the needs of his beloved country in an area so alien to him. Probably it was not that alien to his spirit after all: his ability to imitate persons, to act out scenes, was recognized by his fellow students. The theater must have endeared itself to him also as a means of propagating ideas to a wide audience. All of his plays are highly tendentious and most outspokenly so. Inspired by the examples of Voltaire and Lessing, he proudly considered such a conception to be in the best tradition of the Enlightenment.

Csokonai translated a considerable number of dramas, mostly from the Italian Metastasio. The translation of Schikaneder's text to Mozart's opera, *The Magic Flute*, underlines his didactive purpose. He must have been familiar with Hungarian school dramas, with the

Viennese musical farce: a mixture of scenes from the world of fairy tales, of *commedia dell'arte*, and of burlesque scenes from low life. He transplanted all these theatrical devices into Hungarian and used them to present a genuine Magyar world with truly native types. There is little or no dramatic conflict and little or no action in his plays: for the baroque poet, drama is spectacle and Csokonai was a baroque artist in this genre.[5] The action, if any, relies on a series of well-presented pictures that carry the message of the drama which was what really mattered to him; and his own performing abilities and playful instincts helped him in organization.

Notwithstanding the abundance of characters from popular life— peasants, Jews, Gypsies—Csokonai was not a plebeian playwright[6] but rather a scholar reaching out for an audience he hoped to educate in refinement and culture. Rococo elements were convenient, since refinement of taste was a central issue. The truly racy idiom of most of his low life characters and the artificial, slow-going, boring style of the more sophisticated by no means indicate Csokonai's preference for the people; all rather reflect the state of Hungarian prose at that time. An excellent observer, Csokonai was able to reproduce the idiom of the common people. However, there was nothing to recreate as far as refined conversation went. The predominance of Latin or German in higher and learned circles—the language of teaching was Latin in Debrecen too—prevented the development of an adequate prose in Magyar with sufficient flexibility to express complex ideas. This is why the language became an important political issue, and this explains the weakness of Csokonai's dialogues on intellectual topics.

Csokonai's first play, a product of his college years, *A méla Tempefői, vagy az is bolond, aki poétává lesz Magyarországon (The Musing Tempefői, or only a Fool Becomes a Poet in Hungary)* was first performed in 1935. The title is self-explanatory, as are all the telling names in all his plays. The drama is about the place of poetry and the poet in Hungary. The brief sketch of the missing last scenes does not disclose their content. *Tempefői*, ends on a note of suspense, tension, and uncertainty or even menace to the main character: the poet Tempefői (Dweller of Tempe), and in consequence, the drama sounds like a strange prophecy about Csokonai's own frustrating career. Symbolically then, the play illustrates the fate of a Hungarian poet in Csokonai's time.

Most of the scenes take place in the house of a well-meaning, respectable nobleman totally uninterested in culture. His two daughters are different. Rozália, in love with the poet Tempefői, has a library of Magyar books, and ardently supports literature in the vernacular. Her father condescendingly tolerates what he describes as his daughter's "childish" interest. Éva enjoys the servant's folktales, but, like the empty-headed suitor, prefers meaningless refinement. There are noblemen of all kinds in the drama, all of them uncultured in their own specific ways: fond of cards, of horses, etc. Penniless Tempefői is waiting for a letter from his mother that might rescue him from his debts. Since the letter never arrives in the finished scenes, the poet is in constant trouble with the German-born printer, Betrieger (Cheater), who recently moved to Hungary and soon discovered that only German and French books would sell among the snobbish and shallow nobility, and those only if they were about insignificant topics, like hats, dogs, costumes, fashion, or paying compliments. While Rozália tries to propagate Voltaire in Hungarian, Betrieger makes money on nonsense books translated from French into German. In such an environment—and that is the message of the play—Hungarian books are put to undignified use; they are used for lighting pipes, they serve as wrapping paper, or as with the Franciscan monks, to kindle fireworks. Tempefői cannot pay his debts to Betrieger, nor could Csokonai ever pay for the publication of his works. Tempefői cannot find a generous patron, nor could Csokonai ever. Even the decent, well-meaning father of the two heroines refuses to help him and gives Tempefői only a miserable handout instead of a supportive sum. The same will occur to Csokonai over and over again. After his expulsion from the College of Debrecen, Csokonai, frustrated, considered for a short time turning to the Roman Catholic Church. Even this is foreshadowed in the drama; Tempefői, abandoned by all, asks the Franciscans for help. They, however, support only religious literature and have no interest in Tempefői's secular writings.

At this point an interesting character is introduced, a messenger of the Franciscans to the poet, friar Köteles, the son of a smith. The name implies obligation. Educated in law during the brief period of enlightened reforms by Emperor Joseph, he was soon "obliged" by his family to become ordained. The product of a short period of tolerance—when there were opportunities to obtain jobs by merit rather than by birth—he is now doomed to a life-style alien to his disposition. In the last act Tempefői pays his debt with a purse received from Rozália. Busy-body Betrieger delivers it to the angry father, and the poet is arrested on the suspicion of spying, an indication of the French spy-hunting atmosphere in the early 1790s.

The subtitle leaves no doubt about the topic which is explored from all angles. First, the main character has to learn that none of the various uses of Magyar books is for reading. There are several discussions about the value of literature in Hungarian. Rozália and Éva argue about folk poetry and the role of women in Hungarian society. Rozália first speaks out in Magyar for intellectually emancipated womanhood; she finds Éva's old-fashioned view of the wife—"an idol dedicated to sensual sporting"—"degrading" (I, viii). Tempefői has an inconclusive argument with the sisters' father, Fegyverneki (a Master of weapons) about the value of national literature. Tempefői fails to persuade the nobleman, very much like Csokonai later failed to attract the attention of the nobility. With the exception of a few enlightened liberals, the bulk of the large landlords made terms with Vienna and imitated foreign mores in total indifference to the nation's needs, while most of the country gentry were uncultured, boorish, or at least indifferent to culture. Tempefői has an unsuccessful argument with Betrieger as well. The German printer is practical: convinced that the nobility would not buy Hungarian literature—something Csokonai was to experience later himself—he refuses to print it. Betrieger, though, concedes that the nobility's attitude is "a shame and infamy in this most wise eighteenth century" (II, ii). There is also a competition between Tempefői and a successful poetaster, catering for the pleasure of the uncultured gentry. Evidently, Csokonai had in mind the many versifiers who, boasting of some meager education from the College of Debrecen, flooded the nearby parishes and country residences with their doggerel.

There is no true action in the drama; the message is all important, and the discussions carry the point. The characters do not develop. This shortcoming of the inexperienced writer ironically became a valuable asset in presenting the horse lovers, the cardplayers, the lovers of fashion and empty compliments in their unchanging stupidity, thus illustrating the stagnation in the country. The drama opens without any exposition, in medias res, with Rozália going straight to the point: "Leaders of my nation, when will you learn to value virtue and bravery according to their merits?" (I, i) The rhetorical question implies wishful thinking, and Tempefői soon realizes this: "miserable nation, your prejudices are enemies of refinement" (III, iv). Since both Rozália and Tempefői are for good taste, Csokonai surrounds them with rococo devices. While she is reading, Rozália's heart is filled with "mirth's nectar" (I, ii). Tempefői's house is surrounded by a garden with a bower. Unfortunately, the cheerfulness that should accompany the pleasant garden scenery is lacking in Tempefői's life. The same was true, of course, of Csokonai. Tempefői's lament, "Gloomy abode of my depressing solitude" (II, i), foreshadows our poet's frustration in later years. The hero's determination to bear misfortune "with a philosophic soul" (V, ii), recalls Csokonai's escape into what he called his "simple philosophy." In the meanwhile, another character, Muzsai (one belonging to the Muses), a poet himself, sums up the contemporary situation most perceptively, stating that being Hungarian equals a preference for fashionable clothes, good horses, cursing, eating, and drinking, and it implies an attitude to "hate knowledge and to help the learned to a death of famine" (III, iv).

Csokonai wrote a second play in Debrecen; it was probably performed at the college. Half of the title is in incorrect French, *Gerson du Malheureux* (for "le malheureux") *vagy az ördögi mesterséggel feltaláltatott ifjú (Gerson du Malheureux or the Youth Found through Devilish Practices)*. The lack of female characters indicates that Csokonai intended the play for an all-male cast. In *Tempefői* Rozália referred to Voltaire's *Henriade* in Hungarian translation, the work of a Debrecen bishop. In *Gerson* the reference is to Rousseau. The protagonist is twenty-six years old, a melancholy misanthrope, without a family. After the death of his beloved, he returns from France to his homeland. Inspired by Rousseau, he says about himself: "I wish to hide myself in a tiny recess of nature that will offer innocent delight" (II, v). His melancholy mood, like Tempefői's frustration, reads like a prophecy of Csokonai's own disillusionment later in his life. Contrasting the gloomy scenes in which Gerson and his servant are involved, Csokonai presents a number of episodes of a burlesque, sometimes of almost vulgar nature about a ghost hunt. In the spirit of the Enlightenment, the edge of the drama is, of course, pointed against superstition. Involved in these scenes are a Jew and a Gypsy, both familiar figures in popular Hungarian literature. Their racy idiom is admirable. Most disturbingly, though, all characters are prejudiced against the Jew. Even the enlightened poet emerges as only halfway tolerant. If indeed, as it is usually believed, Gerson is his mouthpiece, that young man definitely takes the Jew's side and defends him; however, he refers to him as an animal, pleading with the others in these terms, "let the miserable animal go" (II, xii). The Jew, who incidentally behaved dishonestly, will not be mistreated, but he is certainly not treated as equal. For young Csokonai, people were divided into two categories: the literates and the illiterates; in his vision, equality would come through the spread of knowledge. Without refinement people live on an animal level. His contempt was not for social status or for race, but rather for ignorance. Such a view, of course, contradicts Rousseau's teaching about the natural state. There are inconsistencies in the play, but then the age itself was full with such contradictory figures as Voltaire and Rousseau.

When next Csokonai turned to writing dramas, he was already in exile, teaching school, this time in Csurgó. He wrote two plays for educational purposes, and they were presented at commencement and other ceremonies. *A Cultura, vagyis az igaz és tettetett szeretet* (*Culture or True and Feigned Love*) is once more about the cultural situation in the country, and in consequence, is reminiscent of *Tempefői*. As a matter of fact, culture is the hero of the play. Csokonai made definite progress in dramatic construction. The drama does not begin *in medias res* anymore; exposition is not neglected; even action of a sort is developed. However, the emphasis is still on a series of discussions rather than happenings. The play was performed in 1799 with Csokonai himself as an actor of a kind. At a point when a German song is supposed to be played on an instrument, the stage instruction reads: "Professor Csokonai behind the curtain" (II, vi). Since action gets more attention, there is even a slight attempt at building up some sort of conflict. Two suitors aspire for fair Petronella's hand. This well-educated, well-read, intelligent daughter of a cultured "gentleman"—as the text has it—is as well versed in literature as in housekeeping. One of the suitors embodies the characteristics of a young Hungarian as Csokonai would have liked to see the youth of the country. While trying to assimilate foreign cultures, Lehelfi (the name means son of Lehel, one of the Magyar national heroes), true to the heritage implied by his name, supports national literature. The other suitor, a well-traveled dandy, delights in foolishly aping foreign models. The issue, then, is the relationship of the Hungarian heritage and of an adequate culture on the European level: whether to assimilate—as Csokonai wanted and did—or to imitate, as the snobs did. Closely related to the main question was the role of Hungarian national costume.

On the issue of national costume, Csokonai seems to have come finally to a rational conclusion worthy of an enlightened mind: it is not the costume that matters but the man behind the costume. The manager of the estate recalls the day when he took his son to the College of Debrecen. There he found that many widely traveled ministers were wearing the national costume, which did not prevent them from propagating knowledge. With his inordinate faith in the power of the intellect, Csokonai worked out the concept of a progressive, clever, rational nationalism. This idea is presented by Tisztes (Honorable), Petronella's father: "For a learned and wise patriot it is not only fair but also necessary to know neighboring nations. First, however, he should know his own homeland." (I, iv). Unfortunately, rational Lehelfi sees only too clearly that for the time being all cultural intentions are doomed to failure in Hungary.

The conflict of ideas is most obvious in Szászlaki's (Dweller of Saxonland) clash with Tisztes. Szászlaki, the young dandy just back from abroad, wishes to use every possible foreign model in his new home in Hungary. Tisztes has a beautiful garden, but he learned from nature and from good books, not from imitating models. The garden once more becomes a symbol of refinement in a positive sense. Empty-headed Szászlaki is surprised to find a garden of good taste "in villagelike uncultured Hungary" (II,v), an observation that helps us appreciate and understand how much the rococo is part of Csokonai's cultural mission.

Like *Gerson, Cultura* too has a subplot, this time involving a Jew and a hired man, a peasant. There is no Gypsy in the play: those vagabonds were less familiar figures in the west of the country. In this musical comedy there are scenes with ethnographical interest like the swineherd dance, the playing of the bagpipe, and above all the singing of the politically motivated Rákóczi song, reminding the audience of Rákóczi's abortive insurgence against the Habsburgs (1705–1711). The singing of that patriotic song made Count Festetich angry; he was concerned about possible consequences detrimental to the school.

The hired man, a plebeian character, gains greater importance than similar characters in earlier plays. His lack of erudition no longer evokes Csokonai's contempt; he is valued for what he has to offer: the national heritage in song and dance. The Jew, too, is treated differently. To begin with, he does not misbehave, and then, Tisztes' secretary, a learned man, refers to tolerance and to the Jew's usefulness in defense of that person: "To hate the Jew is intolerant"—he says—and he is useful too for collecting junk (I, vii).

Karnyóné, vagyis a vénasszony szerelme (Mrs. Karnyó, or the Old Woman's Love), Csokonai's last play, was also performed in Csurgó by his students. Considered his best, it has been performed several times in the twentieth century. The poet composed the music himself for this first model for a later boom of Hungarian popular plays with

music, dance, and figures from folklife. A well-rounded play, without
obtrusive tendentiousness, it shows a definite improvement in theatrical techniques. With Mrs. Karnyó, a small shopkeeper's widow as
the main character, we are introduced into the world of the emerging
middle class. Her husband supposedly died in the Napoleonic wars.
A sister to Dorottya, Mrs. Karnyó, is after a husband, a young,
empty-headed nobleman who, in turn, is after her money. As soon as
his equally unprincipled rival makes him believe that he has won on
the lottery, the unworthy lover leaves the widow, but not without
cruelly opening her eyes: "Your ladyship is a common shopkeeper, I
am a young cavalier, your ladyship is sixty, a battered, cracked violin
on which not even the devil can play" (II, iii). Frustrated, Mrs.
Karnyó sends her retarded son for poison to commit suicide. A
quackdoctor secretly exchanges the poison for a sleeping powder.
Mrs. Karnyó is believed to be dead; at her "deathbed" the other
characters perform a most amusing pantomine. The two parasitic
dandies commit suicide too. The ending of the play is totally unrealistic. First, the husband returns. Mr. Karnyó gives an account of his
war adventures and praises the bravery of the Hungarians and Aus-
trians in the victory of Mantua. Then, a happy ending is brought
about by a device of Viennese musicals: the fairies appear and bring
everybody back to life.

The most important plebeian character is Boris, the maid; a mixture of a Hungarian peasant girl and of a *commedia dell'arte* stock
character, she is the ancestor of a long line of that type in popular
musicals in Hungary. She is also the first to sing a genuine folksong on
a Hungarian stage:

> Can you hear me, my treasure, in Csurgó?
> Do you know that my home is Komárom?
> Come to Komárom
> Where I shall bathe you in kisses. (II, vii).

Besides Boris, Kuruzs (quackdoctor) also deserves special attention
as he describes his many activities: "doctor, barber, alchemist, /
palmist, chiromancer, / ragseller and tinker, / poet, basketweaver"
(II, vii). This variety of occupations may indicate Csurgó's backwardness as compared to Debrecen with its learned doctors and with a
Csokonai as its poet.

One of the students recites an epilogue. First, he makes the point
that anyone who does not like the play should go for better theater to

London. In this proud acknowledgment the poet-scholar takes credit for the creation of Magyar drama by asserting that only the homeland of Shakespeare could surpass his pioneer venture in backward Csurgó, a place backward even in Hungarian terms. Ample praise is poured on the army, but soon the student, speaking the words written by his professor, reveals himself as a spokesman of "mild" Apollo rather than of "wild" Mars. Giving his youth as an excuse, the boy exclaims: "I could never like the ignorant soldier! I have to learn so that I can serve the armed goddess of wisdom in both ways." The student's tender age is, of course, a valid excuse for preferring school to the military, and even the most ardent supporters of the Habsburg case could have no objection, since the student expresses his willingness to serve in the army when he becomes older. Shrewd Csokonai's last word, however, is not the praise of the victory of Mantua, but the cultural message. The commitment is to wisdom rather than to the sword; in a symbolic act, and as he says good-bye to the audience, the student takes off his sword.

CHAPTER 4

Csokonai's Political Views

I The Early Debrecen Years

A serious inconsistency in Csokonai's political views has been a major concern for Marxist critics in Hungary. There is, indeed, a definite shift from the light images of the Enlightenment to a dark or confused imagery after his expulsion from the College of Debrecen. This personal tragedy coincided with an unfortunate upheaval in the life of the nation: the disclosure of the Martinovics conspiracy. Marxists assert that Csokonai abandoned his previous militant stand and turned conservative, even reactionary. However, the range of possible political positions at any moment of Csokonai's time was a great deal wider and more complicated than critics, who accept only militant answers, would admit. Versatile and flexible Csokonai played on a wide gamut of political approaches, but he considered all of them conducive to the benefit of the nation. Though flexible, he always remained within the position acceptable to a responsible Hungarian intellectual. Also, the Marxists are mistaken in their assumption that young Csokonai in his college years was a consistent, plebeian radical. The many contradictions on such issues as the national costume, social classes, etc., in his writings of that period, refute such an argument. Moreover, if there was a change in Csokonai's assessment of the French Revolution, he was by no means unique in such a reversal. Beethoven revoked his dedication of the *Eroica* to Napoleon. Csokonai's close Debrecen friend, the most plebeian Magyar writer of the age, Mihaly Fazekas, called Robespierre and his followers "Cannibals." [1] In his changing views, Csokonai shared in a broad movement among European intellectuals who were disillusioned by the turn of events in France. The following discussion will concentrate on three main points: first, that the change in attitudes was less dramatic than many critics believe, because Csokonai was never a revolutionary; second, that he was never absolutely consistent on some details; third, that he never wavered on one major issue—his dedication to the welfare of the nation.

For a comprehensive picture of Csokonai's political views in his Debrecen student years his fables, his early mock-epic, as well as his political poetry will be studied. Not even the fables, considered by some the best examples of the poet's radical world view, display consistency. Around 1790, inspired by the events in France and by the atmosphere of national optimism, the young Csokonai tried his hand at fables, the popular moralizing genre of the Enlightenment. He called them animal dialogues, and they may have served as practice and preparation for his dramas, since all of them enact a well-rounded scene. These fables turned into a peculiar literary form in the hands of a poet whose talent lay in the more personal style of true lyric.

"A szamár és a szarvas" ("The Ass and the Deer") is the least equivocal of the fables. The deer not only stands firmly for liberty; he is worthy of it. The ass who casually wandered away from his master and seems to enjoy his newfound freedom, voluntarily returns to secure servitude as soon as winter sets in and he must provide for himself. In his endeavor to make this fable into Csokonai's "Manifesto of liberty," [2] Géza Juhász misses a very important detail. The undisciplined behavior of the ass crying out wildly to all asses to follow him into liberty provokes the more mature and dignified deer into angrily reprimanding the unworthy animal: "Unfortunate, you still wear the filth of your former servitude. Liberty does not consist in noisemaking. You are free as far as you have no master now, but you need a brake on your temper" (II, 25). This statement may explain Csokonai's change of heart about the French Revolution; he may have condoned necessary bloodshed but not violent terror, certainly not as a partisan of the Age of Reason. The ass's return to his master proves the deer right; the ass was not yet mature enough for liberty.

"A pillangó és a méh"("The Butterfly and the Bee") is Csokonai's version of "The Ant and the Cricket." The bee is as good a symbol of zealous, fruitful, well-organized work as the ant, while the butterfly satisfied Csokonai's delight in rococo-pastoral scenery and gentle beauty. The bee is a communal being, community oriented, yet the political implications are not without ambiguity with the bee acknowledging responsibility to both his "fellow hive dwellers" and to his "good king." The Hungarian word for citizen (*polgártárs*)—Csokonai's own creation—consists of the term citizen combined with a term meaning fellow or companion, thus underlining the sharing of equal status in society. The poet must have used this compound very consciously; he made the ass refer to "fellow asses" and the bee to "fellow hive dwellers," an obvious reminder of the French Revolution. On the other hand, the bee is clearly a monarchist, the beehive itself being the perfect symbol for a kingdom. Csokonai, then, did not speak out for a republic! Furthermore, the butterfly is not only beautiful but also idle and lazy. If she behaves and talks like an aristocratic lady, despising the bee for the peasant work and all the rudeness that goes with it, Csokonai does not resent it; on the contrary, he enjoys the butterfly's irresistible feminine charm.

The butterfly's morning awakening is like the levee of a lady at the court of Louis XIV. "I get up from my soft bed and wipe my eyes with my legs. Then I go under the roses and sprinkle myself with rosewater. From here I fly to the lilies, poppies, tulips, and shatter the fine powder—and I gently powder myself" (II, 16–17). So the morning scene goes on, almost reminding us of Belinda's dressing toilet in *The Rape of the Lock*. Suddenly, however, the pastoral turns into an unambiguously and charmingly erotical display of flirtation of two lovers. It is told in the first person by the butterfly: "The game consists in one playful butterfly embracing me with his comely legs and it would be discourteous for me not to do the same; out of sympathy he pokes about and it becomes me to accept it. Out of respect he also kisses me all over and being courteous I have to pay him back double. It's his habit to feel my breast and if he is in the mood, he jokingly turns me over, playfully he falls over me, and the devil knows what he does sporting with me, but I like it . . ." (II, 17). Such passages hardly fit the moralistic tone and intention of the fable; these digressions rather reveal Csokonai's search for his own poetic voice. Furthermore, they demonstrate that politics were not his only concern when writing the fables.

The most controversial animal dialogue differs from the other two which, like all classical fables, treat universal human themes. Not so "A bagoly és a kócsag" ("The Owl and the Egret"), a satirical outburst against empty Hungarian nationalism flaunting the national costume, an attitude the poet severely condemns. Egret feathers on hats were an integral part of the national dress, and in this animal dialogue Hungarian patriots are made responsible for the massacre of innocent and beautiful birds. The moving lament of the egret: "Our only misery is the present Hungarian world . . . Joseph's [the emperor's] death, the Hungarians' patriotism is the egrets' death" (II, 8), indicates Coskonai's sympathies with Emperor Joseph's enlightened reforms and his anger with conservative nationalism. The owl, ironically sitting "in the dark," foretells the nation's future: "I hope the new king and calmer nationalism will bring happier times" (II, 14). The owl's closing words underline Csokonai's loyalty to the monarchy and his sharing in the optimistic mood in 1790. The term "calmer" is the key word to the better understanding of the poet's political attitudes. Gentle by nature and nurtured by a city that learned the useful art of compromise, Csokonai was appalled by extremes of any kind and prone to seek middle-of-the-way solutions. The gentle poet is appalled by violence as shown by his description of the cruel killing off of the egrets: "All over lay the scattered feathers, the blood-clogged eggs of the ransacked nests, the headless necks, the hunger-stricken little ones, rigid, out of their nest." (II, 10).

Entirely alien to the genre of the fable is Csokonai's personal intrusion into the action. The birds notice and overhear a youthful poet desperately imploring his Muse to help him to an egret feather, since "an egret-feather is worth more than a sonnet" (II, 11). Though the poet is disgusted by this "egret-feather patriotism," circumstances make him an unwilling hunter. As a last resort he implores the birds themselves to present him with a feather that he can sell to a wealthy compatriot and buy himself a lute with the money. This simple confession, neglected by critics, helps us better understand Csokonai's political stand. His main objective was the promotion of culture; his calling that of a poet. As a responsible patriot, he did write about politics as about all aspects of life; however, this was not his major concern. As a dedicated poet, he was ready for desperate moves, like egret hunting, in order to further the publication of his works.

Békaegérharc (*The Battle of the Frogs and the Mice*), written in 1791 or 1792, is described by Csokonai himself in his treatise on the epic as a mock-heroic, a travesty in Blumauer's manner of Homer's animal fable (II, 144). In his definition of the genre, Csokonai distinguishes three types of the mock-epic and ranges his early work with the first where the discrepancy between unimportant characters and heroic deeds related in elevated diction is the source of the comic. As a mature poet, at a later date, he felt inclined to dismiss this venture of an eighteen-year-old youngster—as he put it (II, 144).

In 1790 Csokonai wrote a poem, "Az istenek osztozása" ("The Gods' Wrangling") satirizing a dispute on the Olympus and mixing Blumauer's style with the no less vulgar manner of student poetry in vogue at the college. The poem, a preparation exercise for the mock-epic, concentrates on political gatherings. It is hard to pin down Csokonai's target for satire in this poem. The gods' gathering may be read as a satire on the Hungarian diet, on the Debrecen city council, or even on the Debrecen church elders' meeting; the confusing diversity of political allusions makes an unequivocal assessment impossible. In this sense too, this poem, a satire on the Hungarian scene full of contradictions, foreshadows the mock-epic.

The abundance of political implications in *The Battle of the Frogs and the Mice* has led critics to erroneous conclusions about the extent of young Csokonai's commitment to the Fench Revolution. As a matter of fact, this youthful work lacks consistency not only on the ideological level, but also in method and style. He must have had in mind his immediate audience, the student body who enjoyed the Blumauer low style. Csokonai's ingenious idea of dividing his work into portions of tobacco for pipes one, two, three, and four rather than the usual cantos helps to understand the kind of audience for which he was writing. Indeed, by connotation, the tobacco serves as a constant reminder of the worst features of backwardness, boorishness, lack of refinement, of obscene vulgarity in talks among men where tobacco smoke was a constant companion of manly conversation. Even the most elevated epic device, the *deus ex machina*, is lowered to this atmosphere. Vulgarity is abundant. Jupiter first appears on the scene with his chamber pot and later his intervention, the battle-winning thunder, is linked with a most biological activity. At the same time, Csokonai's favorite pleasant rococo style is not lacking either. The size of the animals involved almost invited the poet to excell in his exquisite diminutive scale descriptions. He seemed to have delighted in the rococolike characterization of the mice heroes.

> A feather whistle for trumpet;
> the drum of chamois;
> a sharp needle for saber
> (that one from the women);
> the hat of red poppy;
> the wings of butterflies
> for a bouquet.
>
> The shy dragoons
> wore nutshells for breast plates,
> and the lighthearted footsoldiers
> marched in boots of cherry seeds.

No less remarkable is Csokonai's linguistic invention in the diversity of names; some of them Greek, distorted into Hungarian, others German or Slavic imitations, suggesting Hungary's ethnic variety, but best of all those invented to describe the mice's character and way of life, e.g., Greiver-licker, which by connotation suggests servile behavior.

Only an identification of the mice with Hungarians and the frogs with the French would permit a sustained ideological reading of the satire. This, however, is not the case. At the best, two main episodes, the meetings of the mice and the frogs can be identified as a parody on the 1790 diet and the French convention respectively. Random political allusions occur even in these scenes and the confused allusions turn the epic into an ideological riddle. Hungarian patriotic behavior goes as well with the "French" frogs as with the mice. Csokonai introduced almost all major political issues in the Hungary of 1790, but their confused mixture foreshadows the strange character of his future political poetry; indeed, the confusion truthfully reflects on the actual political atmosphere. Decisions about the right and expedient path to take did not come easy even to professional politicians; a young man, geographically far from the city of diets, Pozsony (Bratislava), from Vienna, from Paris, can hardly have had a clear view.

The plot of the mock-epic is extremely simple. In the "Tobacco Portion" for the "First Pipe" (first canto) we are exposed to the chance encounter of the Frog–king and the Mouse–crown prince at a lakeside. Monarchy then prevails in both animals' world. The Frog proposes to carry the Mouse over the lake, an unfortunate enterprise that ends with the drowning of the crown prince and a promise of revenge. In the exposition a number of political issues are cursorily touched on. In his first question the Frog inquires about the new acquaintance's status: "count, burgher, peasant, or noble." Much to his satisfaction, the Mouse reveals his hereditary privileges. The next issue is exploitation. The Mouse hesitates about accepting the Frog's invitation. He is not ready to give up "pinching." In Hungarian this is a pun, since the same term, *dézsma*, would be used for tithe. The Magyar word also carries the meaning of tapping. Next, the Frog mentions the industry that made his country great. The references to international trade, contributing to the upper classes' apparel, are reminiscent of *The Rape of the Lock* where world trade contributes to Belinda's cosmetic table. In the drowning scene, the Mouse, who formerly conceded to tithing the common folk, reverts in despair to a sad "Rákóczi song." "Kuruc" poetry was sad in nature, but then it is

associated with those who paid the tithe and not with those who
thrived on it. We must reemphasize that such inconsistencies make
the mock-epic an interesting reflection of the confused political scene
without giving any definite clue to Csokonai's attitude.

In the "Tobacco Portion" for the "Second Pipe," the poet presents
the gathering of the mice, assembled to discuss the crown prince's
death. Very soon, the lawmakers forget their reason for being there
and spend five weeks in disputing religion. Protestant Csokonai in
Protestant Debrecen must have been well aware of the Roman
Catholic backlash following Emperor Joseph's death. When they
return to the topic of revenge and war, the king addresses the estates,
asking for sacrifice and giving a good example himself. He promises
four millions which "the common people will pay," a satirical comment on similar addresses by Habsburg monarchs in Hungarian
diets. The mice, preparing for victory, strangely enough sing the
"Mohács song." The disastrous defeat of the Hungarian army at
Mohács in 1526 marked the beginning of the one hundred and fifty
years of Turkish occupation.

In the meanwhile, alerted by that sound of trumpets, the frogs
covened the national convention, a term reminiscent of the French
Revolution. Another reminder is the use of a French name, Mr.
Ambassadeur. He brings the message from the land of the mice. The
participants of the meeting are called "faithful patriots"—a strange
choice since the term "citizen" would have suited the French much
better. The passage describing the frogs' hopes for the future after
victory is the only one with a clear political message. They are
planning to turn their prisoners of war into new citizens (not patriots
this time) of the republic. So far we were under the impression that
both frogs and mice lived in a monarchy. But then, Martinovics
himself, the leader of the abortive conspiracy, oddly enough proposed a Hungarian republic under Habsburg rule. This strange plan
of a mature politican would of itself excuse a young poet's confused
views. If the leading radicals had such confused ideas, how would a
young man be expected never to waver! And under such circumstances what amounted to wavering? The frogs are also planning to
plant a tree of liberty in the new republic of the mice. As the general
enthusiasm continues in what now really seems to be a gathering
identifiable with the French events, one of the frogs proposes the
abolition of the use of "fish language" and the introduction of the
vernacular. Csokonai, who at about the same time wrote an essay on
the use of Hungarian, introduced this Magyar concern and thus

obscured the French character of the assembly. Moreover, the frogs preparing for battle wear cockades on their helmets. Like egret feathers, cockades are symbols of Hungarian nationalism in costume.

In the "Tobacco Portion" for the "Third Pipe," the battle scenes attract the reader's attention. In the multinational army of the mice (an evident reference to the Austrian army) all nationalities except Hungarians display shameful cowardice. In the "Tobacco Portion" for the "Fourth Pipe" a mouse victory seems to be imminent. At this point Jupiter intervenes. Some crabs with guillotines on their legs— again a reference to the French Revolution—arrive, cutting the mice's legs and making them run. So the battle is over. In the last stanza, as often in other impersonal writing, Csokonai digresses from convention and strikes a personal note. In an unexpected departure from the vulgar Blumauer manner, a soft-speaking, gentle Csokonai suddenly speaks up to reveal his only true concern, that of the cultural backwardness of the country:

> We have come to the end. I have finished all
> my tobacco. You see,
> very little of it grew
> on the Hungarian Helicon.
> My lords, you must truly admit
> that the hills of Pindus
> are wild from your neglect.

One last inconsistency: tobacco, which earlier served to remind the reader of Hungary's backwardness, appears in this farewell as a plant growing on the Helicon, the dwelling of Muses.

While a student at the College of Debrecen Csokonai wrote a number of poems with political connotations. Some of his early poems about specific types of people contain a social message. Though most Marxists consider the haughty and the miser as representatives of the slowly emerging middle class, as stereotypes they obviously stand for age-old human vices. Indeed, "A kevély" ("The Haughty"), is rather a satire on a common human weakness than a political indictment of a social class. "Zsugori uram" ("Mr. Miser"), though also a satire on a common human vice, is more specific with its many references to Debrecen. The miser lives in a thatched hut, while

> He owns two palaces on Piac Street
> but he rents them to Serbians.

> In his meager hut, cramped from hunger,
> he mumbles to himself about the high cost of living.

Piac Street was and is the main street of Debrecen. In the eighteenth century, renting houses to aliens who were not permitted to have permanent residences was an excellent source of income. The poem, however, is more moral in tone than political.

Nor are Csokonai's early descriptive poems, which incorporated some social ideas in the manner of Thomas Gray's "Elegy in a Country Churchyard," proof of a radical attitude. In "A földindúlás"("The Earthquake") an ironical appeal to the mighty follows the presentation of devastating casualties. The powerful (king, soldier) and the wise (counselor), who exercise power over millions of lives, are asked to halt the earthquake so that they can earn themselves the peoples' admiration. Their inability to comply reflects on the limitations of their power. The tone of the poem is rather moralizing than revolutionary.

So is that of "A nyár" ("The Summer") with an idyllic picture of simple life echoing Rousseau. But the poet's anger with the rich parasite is sincere: "Garbed as peacocks, gauche owls / pretend day is night." Though he is appalled by "the fastidious idlers, whose god their belly is," Csokonai is reconciled to their punishment: a well-deserved bellyache, while the healthy laborer enjoys the simple cheese and bread. As a matter of fact, the poem ends on an idyllic note with the poet reminding the laborer of his happiness: "Reaper, envious of / your lord's luck, Believe me, you're happier!"

The praise of simple life returns in "A tengeri háború" ("The Seastorm"). A fisherman is so successful in comforting a rich merchant who has lost all his fortune in a storm that the merchant decides to join him. Though progressive and sincere, the fisherman's indictment of man's exploitation of his fellowman and his blatant exposure of civilizations' corrupting effects contain no indication of a revolutionary approach. Says the fisherman:

> Man fares on little
> once he alters wish to need.
> And yet this haughty species of ape
> lusts for the whole world.
> All the animals not satisfying him,
> he turns to own his fellowman as well.
> So man puts man in poverty
> when a show of greatness is his goal,

when his wintercoat
is cut from gold lamé.

Even the most obviously political of the early poems are far from
displaying a revolutionary attitude. Csokonai's only poem that at least
in view of its title can be called revolutionary, "A pártütő" ("The
Rebel"), has its meaning shrouded in darkness and even the date is
uncertain. The poem is nonspecific; it cannot be related to any
historical event. In it the poet distinguishes two types of rebels. First,
there is the rebel who like Hora rises against his country. Csokonai's
disapproval of the Rumanian peasant-leader does not help sustain the
image of an early radical Csokonai. The second type of rebel is a
defender of his country against tyranny; he is given that name by the
nation's enemies so that they can murder him. In the poet's view,
"Who is a rebel, who not, the fatherland should decide." In other
words, in a chaotic political situation, the welfare of the fatherland
should be the only guideline. Obviously, the rebel Csokonai had in
mind was a patriot who was persecuted for being a "rebel."

His very first political poem, written in 1790 at the age of seven-
teen, is clearly patriotic. "Magyar! Hajnal hasad!" ("Magyar! The Day
is Breaking!") is the young poet's enthusiastic answer to the nation-
wide joy and celebration. A highly nationalistic and feudal revolt put
an end to Emperor Joseph's attempt at enlightened reforms but also
to his plans of introducing German as the official language. For a short
time progressive intellectuals joined in the patriotic enthusiasm,
hoping that national and democratic ideals could be reconciled.
Csokonai's poem strikes an unmistakably patriotic note but gives no
specific reason why the nation should feel happy. However, this is not
a fife and drum type of verse; the sustained use of dark and light
imagery links it with the Enlightenment. "A gracious dawn" "sending
out its beam into our dark valley" disperses "the ingrained blind
dusk." After the Martinovics executions Csokonai printed this poem
in his most controversial versified newspaper. By that time, the short
period of hope and light turned into darkness again, and Csokonai
added a few sober lines: "Thus sang a naive Hungarian the other day /
when dreaming about the twentieth century." The poem is nonspecific in its enthusiasm. That the poet became disillusioned by the time
he added his famous two lines is obvious. But his disenchantment is as
little specific as was his enthusiasm. There is no evidence that he
became frustrated with the feudal character of the rise of the nobility
in 1790. All we know is that the poet realizes in sad resignation that

"light," whatever content various political groups had given to it, was not to stay in Hungary after all, and that "the fat hopes," whatever they were, had dwindled away.

No more evidence about a radical attitude can be found in the early Debrecen poem "A magyar gavallér" ("The Hungarian Cavalier"), blatantly contradicting his opposition to flaunting the national costume as seen in his fable. In this poem, written in response to the national jubilation over the return of the crown to Pest, Csokonai seems to condone the conservative stand. The *banderia* ("mounted noblemen"), returning home from the celebration, stopped in Debrecen. The occasion prompted Csokonai to write the poem. An almost fife and drum patriotic kind of poem, "The Hungarian Cavalier" alone would refute suggestions that a sharp change occurred after 1795 in the poet's attitude; it rather convinces us that even at this early secure stage of his sheltered life in the Debrecen College environment, Csokonai was uncertain about the correct answer to the Hungarian dilemma: just how much "Magyar" and how much "foreign" is good for the country? The reference to the cavalier's "Asian red trousers" "displaying his belonging to the bloody Magyar species" underlines this point. The brilliant description of horsemanship in the poem suggests that Csokonai enjoyed writing it. At that time he was under no pressure to go against his convictions in order to please a patron. Either he genuinely identified himself with the prevalent enthusiasm or else he simply enjoyed presenting a Hungarian cavalier with impeccable craftsmanship. If this is the case, some of Csokonai's political poems may not reveal personal convictions.

Because of its political connotations, his very first philosophical poem, an epistle, should be mentioned here. "Horváth Ádámhoz" ("To Ádám Horváth") serves as a decisive argument against critics who tend to separate an early radical stage in the poet's career from a later nationalistic-reactionary one. This epistle is not addressed to any great philosopher of the age, not even to an outstanding figure of the Hungarian Enlightenment but to the poet Ádám Horváth Pálóczi, a former student at Debrecen, associated with an extremely conservative and narrowly nationalistic trend.

This teenager's poem surprises us with a stupendious display of contemporary knowledge; indeed, it is the poet's first attempt at incorporating scientific advances in poetry. In a cursory summary of the current scholarly scene, Csokonai initiates the reader into the ideology of the Enlightenment with names like Bernoulli, Newton, Vieta, Leibniz, Kant, and Locke. The young Csokonai, starry-eyed about the wide world, acquired his surprisingly broad knowledge by the age of nineteen, without having left his native city. In 1795 he made a brief allusion to this fact: "My eyes that were catching the light [in reference to the Enlightenment] in Debrecen exclusively" (II, 804). Csokonai appraises the merits of the senior poet, Horváth, as a patriotic achievement, a sure sign of his concern with the fatherland: "He teaches the forests to speak Hungarian, / makes them ring, reel with verses in the Scythian tongue." With Csokonai, Voltaire's faith in the power of knowledge and of the written world turns into a national issue. Conservative Horváth—not unlike Dugonics in a later poem—becomes a symbol of the Hungarian Enlightenment; he "looks with philosophic eyes on the animated world / where he travels the paths Locke prepared, / braves the shadowy places and the rocky curves." At the end of the poem high praise goes to all who translated from French, German, and English into the vernacular and even more to those who ventured into composing original works in Magyar. Horváth himself, called "the beautifier of our language," embodies young Csokonai's ideal: a dedicated patriot contributing actively to the spread of knowledge in a backward country.

Csokonai's eclecticism makes the poem's tone somewhat unbalanced. The personal touch in references to Debrecen collides with the rococo love-poem device of prying. The Muse's prying on Horváth as he is involved in serious activity causes some incongruity, and the discrepancy between the occasionally conversational language of the epistle and the conventionally rather heavy tone of reflective verse is not satisfactorily resolved. Horváth seems to be "chatting" with Kant, Leibniz, and Locke when discussion would be more appropriate. Also, his "sweet lute" is an ill-fitting instrument for academic topics. Though never resolved, this discrepancy is not seriously disturbing, since Csokonai, a member of the Debrecen group of botanists, strives to create an easygoing atmosphere, a community of knowledgeable people among whom knowledge is a commonly shared part of everyday life. Csokonai's student environment and that of the garden-loving learned friends were indeed such a community. The conversational tone then reflects a situation when talk about serious problems was a part of everyday life. Similarly, the garden imagery, though a rococo device, is also a reference to the home environment of the poet's friends.

Another philosophical poem, "Broughton religiói lexiconára" ("On Broughton's Religious Dictionary"), is Csokonai's first poem to discuss religion as a cultural historical phenomenon. In glorifying translators, it turns into one of Csokonai's characteristically patriotic poems, with the image of the poet "blessing," in the final line, the dust of citizens promoting the common good. Csokonai once more emphasizes that mixture of enlightened and national concerns that was his own ideal and also the short-lived hope of radicals in the early 1790s.

In order to print them in the versified journal addressing the nobility after 1795, Csokonai had to revise and subdue the tone of some of his early Debrecen poems. The difference between the original and the later versions is often used as proof of his change of heart. The favorite example is "A had" ("The Army"). The first version, which starts with a terrifying picture of the destructive power of war, sounds like a fiercely antimilitary poem. The description of people getting ready for fight in the second stanza is not linked with any glorification of heroes; on the contrary, the reversal of the light and dark imagery sounds ironical with "the glittering swords cast / ing / a bright shadow over the on-looker's eye." The soldiers are called "gawdy butchers." In the third stanza the angry poet—in an indictment of mankind's history—questions the merit of courage; a murderer who kills one person is killed, while a marble monument is erected to those who kill on a large scale. Summing up the message of this beautifully structured poem, Csokonai applies his theory to the misfortunes of Hungarian history, calling its chronicles "the butcher's block." In the later version, the second stanza is altered to a specific description of the war preparations of the Hungarian nobility. The third stanza is left out altogether; the poet could not have willingly offended those whose patronage he was seeking so desperately, and the Hungarian nobility was fiercely proud of military virtues. A rather unexpected and improper shift to the playful rococo occurs at the end. The poet, too weak to face the terrifying scenes of war, turns away from "the horrible war trumpet" in order to sound his "silver lute." He still condemns war, though no longer in strong, outspoken terms, but rather in a subdued, gentle way. A frail poet's flight to the "gentle" Muse could not have offended anybody's fighting spirit. The revision of "The Army" into a more subtle poem is no proof that Csokonai betrayed his earlier antimilitary convictions, only a sign of caution under unfortunate circumstances.

II   *The Crisis*

The Martinovics circle clandestinely propagated ideas inspired by the French Enlightenment; they never came to overt action. As the French historian, Gérando put it, it was a question of condemnation of ideas, not of action.[3] Under such circumstances, the open exposition of radical ideas became not only dangerous but outright impossible in the atmosphere of icy silence imposed upon Hungary. Csokonai, the only poet not executed or imprisoned in 1795, himself expelled from the college, was desperately trying to have his poems published: at the same time, he tried to avoid giving offense. In the critical year Csokonai was only twenty-two, a susceptible age when young people should be open to various influences. Moreover, flexibility was a major requirement of the Hungarian political scene. Such a prominent, well-informed and well-trained mind as the brilliant József Hajnóczy, the most outstanding personality among the Martinovics conspirators, confessed to being torn between the duties of the enlightened humanitarian and the patriot. The torment generated in the realities of the insufferable political scene was so complicated that the conflicting priorities were never clarified. Democratic and national aims seemed to be at loggerheads most of the time. If Csokonai was caught up between the two equally respectable goals this was not a sign of weakness of character but rather an inevitable outcome of the situation. If he was contradictory in his views of the world around him, the world defied rational solutions. Since an enlightened Hungary as well as an independent Hungary was close to his heart, a firm stand on either issue may have been a practical impossibility given the complexities of the late 1790s. At least Hajnóczy's own confusion seems to support this argument. This alone should discard any shadow of dual loyalty on the part of Csokonai.

His political poetry bears out his own personal dilemmas. His attitude was shaped by his personal misfortune, by a practical sense of compromise, and by the one principle he never compromised on, his love for Hungary. In 1795 Csokonai had very good reasons for being vulnerable, hypersensitive, and prone to indecisiveness. From being an insider in the family of the college, with a secure place in a congenial community, the circle of students and friends, with a brilliant future almost in hand as a college professor, he became from one day to another an outcast, uprooted, companionless, alienated, lonely, with no future and no place to go. His loneliness was absolute. After the Martinovics trials, cultural and intellectual life came to a complete standstill. Not only was Kazinczy, his poet-mentor, imprisoned, but Csokonai lost contact with the Debrecen group of friends, his best audience ever, and with them went the possibility of an exchange of ideas among peers. Without a frank exchange, complex issues cannot be clarified, and the number of these issues was increasing, confronting Csokonai and the nation with anguishing questions. Whether Csokonai's expulsion from the college was politically motivated or not, since it occurred at the same time, the poet's personal misfortune came to be related to the nation's tragedy; it left the deeply hurt young poet, confused, and alone on the cultural scene.[4]

More sensitive than most people, artists generally react more violently to private and public catastrophies. Heartbroken about having to leave, Csokonai overreacted. In "Búcsú a magyar múzsáktól" ("A Farewell to the Hungarian Muses"), a poem written in anger, despair, and total disorientation, a bitter and frustrated Csokonai intends to break with everything he ever respected and cherished. Indeed, he announces his resolution to give up writing. The poet's sincerity in this moment of ultimate despair has to be questioned. There is not a single allusion or indication in his previous poems or letters that he ever considered wealth important at all. It is the more surprising, then, that he pretends to say good-bye to the Hungarian Muses because they leave the poet poor. His pretended rejection of the Muses suggests bitter self-irony: "A laurel may well have great merit: / it secured eternity to Homer. / But it only fares well to be Voltaire, / if you are a gentleman of Ferney and a cavalier." An outcast, he was evidently unlike Voltaire when he announced his readiness to embrace the legal profession. "Perhaps they won't bite me"—he says in an unmistakable reference to recent painful incidents. However, he is severely honest about his disgust for that profession, calling lawyers people "who stir the legal juice into a pig-wash." The poem is a frustrated and bewildered reaction to the sudden misfortune. Csokonai was literally excommunicated and even forbidden to enter the college; students were forbidden to talk to him (II, 799). No wonder he was considering suicide. The only alternative was to go to the College of Sárospatak where he was invited to study law. Dislodged, shifted to strange surroundings, the vulnerable and insecure Csokonai tried to filter the confusing and disquieting flood of events through his mind and to give them some coherent shape in his poetry. Any hesitancy or shift in his attitudes should be judged against this background.

Csokonai was well-trained in compromising by the tradition of his native Debrecen, a proud Protestant city that had learned to survive by wisely accommodating in an often painful and humiliating manner the contradictory wishes of Muslim Turks and Catholic Habsburgs. A passage from the 1790 town council minutes describes how the city "had been conserved . . . by bowing its head and adjusting itself."[5] This is exactly what Csokonai was trying to do. Adjusting became a way of life for him when for the next few years he moved from one friend's house to the other's in the capacity of a "professional guest." No one can be a welcome guest for any length of time without giving up something of himself. The problem is what and how much. No wonder then that Csokonai became a violent attitudinizer. He was helped in this performance by his theatrical ability as well as by his early training in writing poems on given rather than chosen themes. One of the attitudes he strikes, probably the only sincere one, is that of everybody's poet, the nation's poet, and such an attitude demands a capacity to identify with various stands. Those who are so hard on him and ready to judge him should not forget that Rousseau himself was compelled to accept a lackey's job at a certain period of his life.

In all his wavering attitudes, Csokonai never shifted the emphasis from the basic issue: the good of his beloved country. If—as some believe—he was indeed present in the crowd watching the execution of the Martinovics conspirators, he described this participation not as a revolutionary but rather as a patriotic manifestation. In his poem "Mátyási József úrnak" ("To Mr. József Mátyási") he described the company traveling to Pest in 1795 as "our beloved country's / true sons." If caution made him choose the term, it certainly agreed with his convictions. Patriotism was the issue he emphasized in his "Búcsúzó beszéde a debreceni kollégiumi ifjúsághoz" ("His Farewell Address to the Students of the College of Debrecen") recommending loyalty to the country as one of the major virtues; besides patriotism, he cited love of the fellowmen (enlightened humanitarianism) and the love of knowledge (II, 791–96).

While in Pest, Csokonai visited András Dugonics, a university professor who lectured in the vernacular. The poem "A Dugonics oszlopa" ("The Dugonics Monument") is often cited as an indication of Csokonai's betrayal of enlightened ideals or at least of disorientation. András Dugonics was the leader of a conservative, highly nationalistic group of poets and the author of the first best-seller in Hungarian literature, *Etelka* [a female name], a naive and poorly written historical novel glorifying the nation's past. But the conservative nationalistic attitude was not entirely new to Csokonai; he glorified it in "The Hungarian Cavalier." What constitutes a departure from his previous stand is that the disappointed poet does no longer look into the future as the enlightened attitudes require but, in a rather romantic fashion, turns to the national past and hopes to find solace in past glory. The structural and stylistic disharmony in the poem may be interpreted as an indication of profound confusion but it may also be a clever and deliberate device. As the poem begins, the poet is contemplating his favorite diminutive world of "tiny violets and forget-me-nots," most unbecoming to the historical theme when suddenly he notices the monument. In shocking contrast to the rococo environment he observes "a huge obscure cave" covered by "ancient moss," "dusky clouds," and a "fog-curtain." These images of darkness could be a deliberate device signaling the poet's unwilling departure from his rococo world into the darker realities of the present and indicating quite accurately Csokonai's uncertainty about his own and the nation's future. The poem is not depressing though. At the end Dugonics is praised a "great scholar" and "a citizen with a Hungarian heart." The word "citizen" has strong and very specific connotations; for Csokonai it meant a close identification with enlightened ideas. The real Dugonics was a man "with a Hungarian heart" but certainly not a citizen in that sense. Not unlike Ádám Horváth in Csokonai's early philosophical poem, the real Dugonics is transformed into our poet's ideal Hungarian, a knowledgeable intellectual and progressive patriot. In view of this similarity, "The Dugonics Monument" far from demonstrating undue hesitancy, rather confirms the poet's consistent approval of the 1790 alliance of nationalistic and progressive forces. Such an alliance may have also satisfied the spirit of compromise by which his native Debrecen had learnt to survive. However, Csokonai's unconscious realization of the incongruity between conservatives and progressives may explain the structural unbalance and stylistic disharmony in the poems about Dugonics and Horváth, conservative nationalistic figures whom he turned into progressive patriots.

The poem "Oh, szegény országunk" ("Alas, Poor Country of Ours"), imitates in content, manner, and style the rebellious "kuruc" poetry of the Rákóczi War of Independence. It is also patriotic; if there are any social connotations, they are linked to anti-Habsburg attitudes. The poem starts with a lament, a "kuruc" convention:

> Oh, our pitiful country,
> Oh, our poor homeland.
> No longer free,
> the yoke on our neck—
> Where do we go? and what do we do now,

> now we are so fettered?
> Go to another country?
> To a country without a tyrant - why not?

The suggestion of exile is in the "kuruc" tradition, too, and so is the fierce hatred of Germans in almost all the five other stanzas. The Germans are called "the lowest and scum" of mankind. After the defeat of Rákóczi's fight, the Habsburg supporters, the "labanc" received huge estates as recompense for their loyalty. Similarly, in Csokonai's time favors and rewards went to aliens loyal to the Habsburgs.

> Unless from the Viennese
> (that fox) we beg,
> a grand estate
> is denied the Hungarian.

Csokonai accuses the Habsburgs of turning Hungary into a colony, "wicked serpentlike suck[ing] / its honey and milk." The lines

> If the Hungarian has a heart,
> if he shows a will,
> to the headsman's sword
> he will fall victim . . .

may be a reference to the Martinovics executions. Yet it is important to remember that in the context of a "kuruc"-like patriotic poem the issue is not social or political revolution, but the independence of the fatherland.

Not all the post-1795 poems are more compromising in tone than earlier ones. "Az én vagyonom" ("My Fortune") treats the rich versus poor issue in a more emphatic way than any early descriptive poem. Csokonai's anger with, and contempt for, those, who in order to secure financial well-being, are "crawling in the dust" and become "servants to others" are much stronger here. Far from seeing himself as selling out, Csokonai dissociated himself from those who did. As in the milder version of "The Army" where Csokonai turns to his gentle lute, at the end of "My Fortune" the poet escapes into a pastoral setting. There he finds delight "with the singing birds." This poem, overlooked by critics, is indeed a crucial one. It suggests the beginning of the poet's involuntary withdrawal from a world that was becoming increasingly unbearable. In this sense, this poem, so much more personal than others of the same period, contains a frustrated poet's personal response to, and indictment of, the contemporary Hungarian scene.

III After 1795

The main concern of contemporary Hungarian critics is Csokonai's controversial versified newspaper, A diétai magyar Múzsa (The Diet's Hungarian Muse). A failure in the moral and financial sense as well, this strange enterprise stands as a clear proof of Csokonai's flexibility, expediency, and his sad realization that resistance was wasteful. The penniless, homeless, jobless Csokonai launched this newspaper in the hope of securing the benevolence and material support of the nobility assembled in Pozsony (Bratislava) for the 1796 diet. The idea of a Maecenas, common at the age, was not new to the poet. In a poem, written as a school exercise, he wrote in the hope for the revival of Hungarian letters: "If only a Maecenas our country could produce." Moreover, Csokonai cannot be condemned by any reasonable standard for identifying with the nobility. Though he never associated himself with their reactionary fear for their privileges, his own family claimed noble rank. Furthermore, Csokonai's ignorance about the aristocracy cannot be discounted either. Since he had no firsthand knowledge of them among Debrecen's peasant-burghers, the young poet's image of the magnates must have been based on their fame and their important role in the nation's life. The introductory poem "A főtiszteletű, méltóságú és tekintetű Rendekhez" ("To the Right Reverend, Right Honorable, and Honorable Estates") displays a sincere and naive faith in those "glorious persons," destined to be "the fathers of our great nation."

The weekly issues contain slightly modified versions of poems considered progressive if not radical, like "The Evening," "The Army," "Magyar! The Day is Breaking!" as well as "Mr. Miser" and "The Earthquake." The altered texts—as discussed earlier—show no betrayal of enlightened ideals, just prudent caution. Some new poems, however, indicate a more disturbing attitude. "A mostani háborúba vitézkedő magyarokhoz" ("To the Hungarians Gallantly Fighting in the Present War") not only contradicts the antiwar tendency in the first version of "The Army," but contains a strong indictment of the French Revolution as well. The easy flowing, impeccable hexameters do not show a lowering of standards that some critics pretend to detect in these poems. Like so many other poets all over

Europe, Csokonai changed his attitude to the French Revolution. He refused to condone bloodshed in "The Army" just as, a few years later, he refused to accept the bloodshed of the Terror. Was he inconsistent?

The strangest poem of the whole collection is "Az 1741-diki Diéta" ("The 1741 Diet"). This puzzling cantata in nine songs mixing baroque, classical, and operalike elements, reviews Hungarian history from 1741 to 1796 in the form of a prophecy. This poem, indeed, is a full-length exercise in head-bowing, overpraising not only the nobility but also the Habsburgs. Of course, praise went also to enlightened Emperor Joseph, a favorite of the poet's father and appreciated by Debrecen Protestants. Indeed, this promoter of tolerance is likened to the most popular of all Hungarian kings, Matthias Corvinus (1458– 1490), nicknamed the Just, a friend to the poor and the oppressed. But Joseph is by no means the only Habsburg receiving praise in this poem. The overall picture presented by the versified newspaper is certainly confusing, yet it reflects adversely not so much on the uprooted, grief-stricken young poet as on the hopelessly confused political realities. His preface, where he apologizes for his Muse's total ignorance in matters politics as well as for the Muse's naive desire to please everybody (II, 128), is rewarding reading to all who are hard on Csokonai for his political jugglery.

The total failure of the versified newspaper, the nobility's complete indifference, did not break him down. His admirable resilience took him to Komárom where the nobility assembled in 1797 responding to the emperor's call to rise against Napoleon. "A nemes magyarság felűlésére" ("On the Rise of the Noble Magyardom") begins with a farewell to the light Muse of "innocent sports" and of "wreaths of hyacinth." Though resolute to "shatter Parnassus with drum and trumpet," Csokonai is not himself ready to fight; he rather offers to accompany the army as a trumpeter. There is no derogatory attitude to the war, no "butcher's block" mentality. Instead of classical hexameters he chose the twelve syllable lines, popular in Magyar poetry glorifying military virtues. This choice as well as the many powerful images are certainly no evidence of lack of aesthetic standards. Csokonai had an excellent training in writing a good poem on a given proposition. No dishonesty was therefore involved when, hard pressed by circumstances, he seemed to stand on both sides of an issue. He had been trained to write convincingly for various opinions. Also, he was a first-rate actor, capable of identifying himself with a role and acting it out to perfection. In consequence, it is hard to decide whether in this particular poem he was merely trying to please the nobility or whether he himself considered war justified at this point. If he felt he had to condone war, he certainly did so with a heavy heart.

Whatever his feelings, Csokonai was relieved when the fighting was over. Celebrating the peace of Campoformio, he wrote an antique ode, "A békekötésre" ("On the Conclusion of Peace"), emphasizing the dire consequences of war, the immeasurable private and public sufferings. The poet refers to his personal hardships but more importantly to those of his "forlorn country." In view of his concern for the fatherland, this poem ranks with Csokonai's best patriotic ones. It is also a characteristically enlightened poem, in which the land at war with its "rude heroes" is contrasted to the land of peace "where the sage instructs and the poet sings." Csokonai, attracted by the land of the sage and the poet, is ready to return to his gentle Muse:

> With the roar of great guns around me stilled,
> I can hear the banter of my friends,
> and with my delicate lute, I sing farewell
> to trumpet and drum.

Torn between lute and trumpet, Csokonai will strike a puzzling note once more with "Az igazság diadalma" ("Justice's Triumph") in 1799, celebrating the victory of Mantua. Goya-like, nightmarish images of war evoke the poet's disgust for the fanatics of the Terror; Csokonai calls the people in revolt "scum" and "many-headed monster," "whose freedom blooms in a withered tree, / for whom equality is a red cap," who betrayed the ideals of liberty and equality and ultimately "crushed the rights of men and nations." The poem comes as no surprise, though, in the context of an almost universal frustration among European intellectuals over the turn of events in France. Even the praise of the four monarchs fighting against Napoleon makes sense against such a background. What Csokonai really objected to may well have been the crushing of the Enlightenment's ideals by bloody events and the emerging power of Napoleon. If so, Csokonai, in turning against the French Revolution, was more loyal to his youthful enthusiasm for those ideals than many critics are willing to admit.

Csokonai's only noncontroversial political poem of the post-1795 period is "Jövendőlés az első oskoláról Somogyban" ("Prophecy on

the First School in Somogy"), written in 1799 while he was a substi-
tute teacher in Csurgó, County Somogy. The poem consists of a series
of unanswered questions, all of them about the reasons for backwardness. Since the accused are never named, the poem is politically
harmless. The speedy sequel of short questions and brief statements
lends the poem a peculiar kind of urgency conveying convincingly the
poet's anger and his appeal for fast action. As any thinking person
could learn, those responsible are the same "glorious fathers of the
nation" and that very emperor whom he praised not much earlier for
defeating the French:

> How many good minds grew wild,
> being uncultivated?
> How many a citizen became a boor,
> without good learning?
> A weed among weeds
> a pineapple would become.
> The ignorant man will be a dolt
> if his teacher is a boor.
> Seeing that
> Somogy
> is so ignorant,
> uncultured,
> whom can we blame?

The poem ends on a vague note of hope pushed into a vaguely
described future.

To end this survey of Csokonai's political poetry, his occasional
poems with political connotations must be assessed. Most of those
were written to prominent magnates whose patronage he hoped to
gain. We know from his preface to "Alkalmatosságra írt versek"
("Occasional Poems") that he questioned the aesthetic qualities of
most (II, 229). Nevertheless, he hoped to publish them either for the
significance of the topic or out of gratitude. There is no dismissal for
reasons of content. On the contrary, he mentions topics of importance. Indeed, those magnates whom Csokonai was asking for support were the most eminent members of the Hungarian nobility, the
worthiest, men such as Czindery, the alleged translator of Rousseau's
Social Contract into Latin; Festetich, the founder of the Georgikon,
the country's first and still foremost agricultural college; and
Széchenyi, the protector of Hajnóczy executed for participating in
the Martinovics conspiracy. Széchenyi later founded the National

Library that bears his name. If they occasionally cautioned Csokonai, they had every reason to do so; they knew better than to encourage useless resistance. If they failed to recognize the genius of Csokonai, of this young bothersome, ragged, ugly poet, at least they did not fail the nation entirely under extremely adverse circumstances. If Csokonai, the poet of the Enlightenment, wrote a poem in praise of the founder of the National Library, if in a letter (II, 909) he praised Széchenyi for his "unmatched sacrifice" for the advancement of learning, can Csokonai be accused of overpraising? The library was a major contribution to the cultural elevation of Hungary, and that was Csokonai's only continuous concern. His attitude, then, was not merely patriotic but also enlightened in the eighteenth-century meaning of the word. Csokonai was a comprehensive poet in many ways; he tried out various styles and many attitudes. He also projected a comprehensive view of the Hungarian scene; such a picture certainly included the nobility in a country where they had the only voice, and where one person in ten claimed gentle status.[6] Furthermore, a nobility that also produced a Festetich and a Széchenyi cannot be dismissed as reactionary as a whole.

In a country where public affairs were closely linked with national culture, the poet's survival as a poet depended on politics. Though an unstained idealist to the end, in a period of disenchantment for him as well as for the nation, Csokonai had to try to practice the politics of possibility and had to turn some times into an egret hunter himself. The most disturbing political act was an application in Latin to Emperor Francis in 1796, asking for a small estate that he could cultivate for himself. In exchange he offered "such service by which I could recommend myself and the Hungarian Muses to prove my fullest loyalties" (II, 1035). If we examine Csokonai's political views in the terms of his three main principles—patriotism, enlightened humanitarianism, and love of knowledge—we find little inconsistency; he never wavered on those. If we consider Csokonai's application to the emperor in this context, we can assess it as part of the traditional Debrecen head-bowing exercise, a shrewd act of compromise. A piece of land would have given the poet the opportunity to dedicate all his energies to the Muses, and even the most militant critics concede that after 1796 the only possible political activity in Hungary was in the cultural field.[7]

Throughout his life Csokonai tried to serve as a patriot by being the poet he was born to be. The integrity of his poems was his main concern, and he tried to protect them from censors by declaring that they were not "against the throne or the altar"; more emphatically, he asserted that "For all the world I do not want to mingle in the affairs of the state" (II, 950). His business was not politics but poetry. If in a letter he declared that he did not need political freedom and that he could live under any sort of European or Oriental tyranny as long as it did not hurt his body, this is no sign of reactionary attitude. "My soul"—he wrote in the same letter—"is above and outside their sphere, it is only mine" (II, 975). A poet so proud, so confident of his integrity could not have seen himself as having shifted irresponsibly on major issues.

CHAPTER 5

Csokonai's Philosophy

I Great Philosophical Poems of the Enlightenment

BETWEEN the ages of nineteen and twenty-one Csokonai produced almost all of his so-called philosophical poems, his major
achievement aside from the love lyrics. Written during that very
short period of hope when progressive democrats joined forces with
conservatives, Csokonai's philosophical poems deal in an aggres-
sively affirmative way with the major issues of what he himself called
this "century of philosophy" (II, 238). The themes, all of universal
human significance, favored a moralizing impersonal tone. Yet this
community-spirited public poetry differs significantly from similar
Western-European poems. Such great issues of mankind as religion,
liberty, equality, and the spread of knowledge, emerge here against a
specifically Hungarian background. As in other Eastern-European
literatures of the same period, a strongly national concern dominates
all these poems. Csokonai approaches the almost commonplace
themes of the eighteenth century from a Hungarian, sometimes even
Debrecen point of view. In twelve-syllable couplets, skillfully em-
ploying language and imagery, the poet conveys his ideas with
magnificent power. Most of these poems developed out of the two
types of early school exercises for his poetry class. The moralizing
poems merged with the descriptive ones; the latter served as the
foundation to which, in accordance with the requirements of the Age
of the Enlightenment and also with the Puritanical, serious, morally
conscious spirit of the college, and in keeping with the role of the
illuminate poet, message-carrying passages were added.

In this age of depersonalized poetry, when lyrics were not really
practiced or appreciated, Csokonai, a lyricist by disposition, not only
raised the genre of reflective poems to its highest peak in Hungary,
but also enriched that poetry with a personal tone, indicative of the

coming romantic period. In the guise of a conventional genre, he managed to create an individual form of expression, a kind of poetry in which the almost scholarly documented treatment of the great issues of the Enlightenment coexists with a tone that may be sometimes strikingly and almost disturbingly personal.

The European Enlightenment was a complex movement, and so were Csokonai's views embracing the heritage of both Voltaire and Rousseau. On the one hand, as a true admirer of Voltaire, the Hungarian poet believed in the power of reason, of knowledge, of the written word as conducive to that happy state of mankind when man, that rational being, will learn how to organize and preserve a happy and well-balanced life for all humanity. Embracing Voltaire's faith in the educational force of knowledge, Csokonai made the creation of culture his main objective; even his view of democracy was culturally conditioned. For him, democracy meant a situation of shared cultural values, of the kind he enjoyed at the college, where the commonly shared school training eliminated the differences between sons of gentry and peasantry. Such an outlook explains Csokonai's ambiguous attitudes toward illiterate lower classes who, at least in his early dramas, are treated with some condescension. On the other hand, Csokonai was also familiar with Rousseau, who distrusted that very reason on which Voltaire based his hope for the future of mankind. Rousseau believed that compassion and the ability to identify are necessarily much more perfect in the state of nature than in the state of society. Indeed, in his view, the "reason" of men in society engenders self-love. Csokonai made skillful use of the inherent contradictions in the philosophy of the Enlightenment as represented by these two men. He relied on their thinking and teaching as circumstances dictated. Such a practice contributed to the shift in tone of his poetry discussed in the previous chapter. After 1795, with all the heartbreak of national and personal life, he found Rousseau more and more attractive, but he never entirely turned his back on Voltaire. In one of his letters he made this ambiguous statement: "Only the book and the coffin can reestablish the original equality among men." The book, of course, is a reminder of Voltaire. However, Csokonai realized that a due appreciation of books would come in a distant future only, "when Nature [Rousseau's ideal] will raise its all-mighty word," and when people "will feel, think, and love" (II, 810). Into this disharmonious combination of the natural state with books, of thought with love, merged Csokonai's concern with Magyar issues. All this combined constitutes the background of his reflective poetry.

One of Csokonai's major reflective poems, "Az estve" ("The Evening") opens with a quiet, peaceful evening landscape, thus enabling the poet to present his deep philosophical ideas in a lighter tone. The unusually nervous rhythm, four three-syllable beats in the traditional twelve-syllable couplets, reflects the poet's personal disquietude. The soft, gentle language of the introduction contradicts the angry tone that carries the social message in the bulk of the poem. Throughout the poem, the poet is personally involved in the intellectual argument; throughout the poem his argument is emotionally conditioned.

In the all-pervading peace, suggested by the opening stanza, even the wild beasts keep quiet. In the second stanza the poet himself becomes part of the calm evening atmosphere that seems to exclude grief and where all the senses enjoy themselves in graceful company of sweet night music, fair breezes, heavy scents, and moonshine. Yet it is not a merry place after all but rather one of "cheerful melancholy." This paradoxical term, calling to the mind Andrew Marvell's much stronger "magnanimous despair," marks the turning point in the poem. The mild pastoral tone changes; the poet becomes overwhelmed with anxiety. If earlier he was ready to enjoy the evening scene, now he fears approaching night's "cold wings." They are not so much a reminder of death—as the reader would expect—than of Csokonai's alienation from society. The poet is getting tired of "the world's noise" and "the haughty and miser's rattling." An uneasy Csokonai foretells the crowded loneliness of our century: "As people are teeming around me, / they crowd each other, drunk with appetite." Yeats' beautiful line about the soul "drunk with desire" comes to mind. The next stanza, carrying the ideological message, exposes Rousseau's ideas in his *A Dissertation on the Origin and Foundation of the Inequality of Mankind*. The social evils disclosed explain the poet's feelings of alienation, yet in the long fourth stanza the personal tone is less strong. Mankind, created free, later fettered its own hands. In declaring property the root of evil, Csokonai echoes Rousseau's view that the first person who said about an enclosed piece of ground, " 'This is mine' and found people simple enough to believe him, was the real founder of civil society." [1] There is no more specific indictment of social inequities in our poet's whole *oeuvre* than these words about the natural state: "There were no beggars made by law, / and nobody was born rich, nobody poor." As Csokonai proceeds with his discussion of lords and peasants, the condemnation of exploitation takes on a Hungarian coloring with the word *dézsma*, a term for a certain kind of tithe. Then the poet's thoughts return to nature. This nature, however, is different from the peaceful evening scenery of the opening; this is nature misused by man where

> Now the long furrows are gashes in the meadow.
> In the forests, the lord's fences
> keep the lord's game, a private collection.
> The poor have been made to plant the very trees
> that block the water back from them.

The last stanza, with a touch of the idyllic, calls to mind the equivocal nature of pastoral poetry. The shepherd and the laborer still seem to enjoy "the golden moonlight," "the life-giving air," "the forest's sounds." The sad but quiet note of resignation at the end justifies the paradoxical term "cheerful melancholy," as a disillusioned Csokonai confesses his preference for the natural state over the civilized:

> Blessed nature, oh, you are my only
> possession, my only property,
> whose eternal landlord I became
> as soon as through you I was born a man.

The twin poem to "Az estve," "Az álom" ("The Dream") relies much more on Voltaire. The emphasis on reasoning, on logical argument, forms the base for the convincing reflections. If the evening scene reminded the poet of inequities in society, the dream reminds him of death and of the philosophical ideas related to it; both pleasant and frightening dreams revigorate soul and body. They are beneficial, since by making us almost dead, they deliver us from life's troubles:

> That's it, make us dead. Our living,
> is proved by a slight breath.
> So when will this little breathing cease too?
> When will sleep itself sleep?

The logic seems perfect. Death appears a brother to sleep, and the young poet, trying to liberate man from the fear of death, enjoys the discovery of this simple and pleasant truth. The major section of the poem consists of an unequivocally materialistic discussion of life. Under the influence of Diderot and Holbach, whose writings Csokonai was translating at that time, the poet refers to the hope of life after death as "the obscure dreams of the living." "Since what was nothing, becomes again nothing; / our body's dusty frame becomes earth." The description of the process of decay of the body, in shockingly naturalistic terms and in minute details, ends with the corpse's becoming useful and nurturing again. Csokonai makes his argument more convincing by introducing an illustrative example, the fertile wheat-growing region of Bánát:

> Even Bánát, soaked with the blood of humans,
> the bodies of Hungarians and Turks its compost,
> holds such rich grass, that smelling it
> repulses even the grandest horse.
> And thus it is that the living becomes mineral and soil,
> The bloated corpses of the living become growing plants
> which are eaten by animals
> that in turn are nourished and grow.

In the context of this continuous cycle, the individual human life dwindles into insignificance. In the closing lines, though, the poet becomes personal: the talk is no more of man in general, but rather of Csokonai himself, as a part of mankind, and of the whole eternal circle of beings:

> What was I before birth,
> before I took this body from grass and animal?
> I was deep asleep in the quiet, peaceful night
> where in different form I knew not what I was
> until I became a living man;
> and finishing that form, I shall return,
> decomposing to something else,
> a tiny part of nature.
> After my coffin? I imagine I am
> the same that was before my cradle.
> I go to sleep, the long sleep, rotting
> to a collection of nutrients.

The poem "Konstancinápoly" ("Constantinople") evolved from an early school exercise describing a city. Voltaire and other writers of the age resorted to the Orient as a convenient device for moralizing purposes. Csokonai's poem reads like an attack on religions in general in the guise of an indictment of Islam. It also contains his brightest, most optimistic prophecy about mankind's future.

Csokonai invites the Muse on a sightseeing tour. The reader is shown around in the noisy, colorful, impressive, thronging Oriental city. We enjoy the tumultuous scene and the easy conversational style, but Csokonai hastens to remind us that all those teeming people conform "to a single order." Of course, he has Islam in mind but implies all fanatical systems. Suddenly a veiled woman appears, and the poet resumes his playful mask, guiding the reader into the sultan's harem, compared in the young student's erotic fantasy to a library full of books, all ready and willing to open up if the sultan so desires. Frightened by a eunuch, the poet rushes his readers into the street.

The view of the magnificent mosques provokes Csokonai into a fierce attack on religion. Since light for the poet of the Enlightenment has a clarifying and purifying power, religion appears in images associated with darkness, hiding light from man. "Oh, what thick cloud has been cast over these people" by "superstition! owl bigotry!" From Voltaire, Csokonai turns to Rousseau, as he invokes the natural state where "This world was happy, and the vain word Sacred / did not help excuse terrible evils." In the civilized state pompous temples came to be built by "numbed reason," again a term that would have pleased Voltaire. Csokonai stays with Islam all through the poem; yet a few allusions to Friday fasting, liturgies, and asceticism unmistakably refer to Christianity. Suddenly the poet is carried away by a vision of the future and goes into raptures about what reason can achieve: "Rise, my soul. Even now I see a time / when reason will cry out / and at once the dark curtains will part. . . ." In powerful images Csokonai describes bells ringing for happiness and announcing the good life when—again with reference to Rousseau—compassion triumphs and "man embraces man again." Though the confusion is undeniable, Csokonai is reasonable enough not to hope for an early realization of this state of nature brought about by reason, undoubtedly a strange combination:

> Hurry on proscrastinating century. Come, happy age!
> Though I'll be soulless dust by then,
> I'll still herald your arrival in song.
> If only once you would remember me,
> then though this owlish world may frighten me with death,
> I would die in noble disgust.

In this, his most optimistic philosophical poem, Csokonai qualifies his optimism by the personal note of "noble disgust," and makes us

wonder how far the young poet's optimism was genuine and undis-
turbed even at this early sheltered stage of his life.

"Marosvásárhelyi gondolatok" ("Thoughts on Marosvásárhely") is
the most Hungarian of his major reflective poems. The inspiration
was the founding by György Aranka, in 1793, of the first Hungarian
scholarly body—the Linguistic Society of Transylvania—dedicated to
the cultivation of the vernacular. Once more the starting point is a
landscape, this time the natural beauty of Transylvania. The poet's
mind, "fully filled with the image of my sweet country," as he puts it,
rambles freely over the fate of nations, "now rejoiced, now grieved as
a citizen of the world." Csokonai's humane and patriotic concerns
dominate every line of the poem, a poignant confession in terms of
contemporary philosophy of Csokonai's realization of Hungary's key
position between East and West.

The poem is about mankind and, since Hungary is part of it, it is
more specifically about Hungary's place among nations. In a perceptive sensitiveness to the issue of race, Csokonai considers the earth's
population as "the black and white inhabitants of the same house."
The almost certain extinction of Magyars left behind in the Asian
homeland brings Csokonai to think that sometime in the future "the
site of Paris will be carefully searched / by scholars now sifting
Babylon, Troy; / and seals will swim through the windows of London." Such passages, far from radiating Enlightenment optimism,
almost anticipate Spengler. However, the continuous Hungarian
anxiety about national survival well explains the poet's outlook. He
was deeply disturbed about whether the kinless Hungarian language
could survive another century. As soon as he asks himself the question why some nations are free and some slaves, he comes up with a
typical Enlightenment phrase as an answer: "Vile ignorance! unre-
strained passion" account for "the cloud of superstition," while reason
and knowledge, of course, are conducive to good life. The poet soon
returns to his main concern, the place of Hungary:

> The most critical spot on the world's map—
> set between comley West and rough East,
> the mighty North and the passive South,
> Being so in the center, it illustrates
> the nature of man and of earth.

To the east of the nation there are the savages, "the still unhappy
half-men." In this poem Csokonai disregards the benefits of the

natural state he so much admired in others. He identifies the condition of "brown people," who are still in the barbarian stage, as evil; while the civilized condition of the Germans, French, Peruvians, and Bostonians, is characterized as good. In consequence, "Then, Oh Maros's devout castle, you stand / where the frontiers of good and evil meet; / you are the point where savagery is tamed." In this anti-Rousseauesque poem, reason is the answer. "Beware. The reef of darkness is close / enough to wreck you, unless reason's beacon guide your way." The last section contains an appeal to Hungary, in terms of the philosophy of the Enlightenment, to join the civilized nations of Europe. Although the theme is constant in Magyar poetry, Hungary has never been more heartbreakingly described as the last bastion of European culture than in this poem. Csokonai strongly believed that his kinless nation's survival depended on its close association with the culture of Western Europe, without giving up the national identity. Csokonai's own achievement as he Magyarized the ideas of the Enlightenment is an excellent illustration of this process. There is much truth in Géza Juhász' observation that all the early philosophical poems have a definite elegiac tinge to them,[2] but without convincing evidence we cannot accept his explanation that the poet's gloomy mood was caused by his knowledge about the disclosure of the Martinovics conspiracy. The elegiac attitude may better be attributed to the poet's qualified optimism and hope for a brighter future of the Hungarian nation. This is why he was so inconsistent in his references to Voltaire and Rousseau. Such a wavering attitude over the three of four years in the most stable period of his problem-stricken life, makes his hesitating attitude over political issues after the expulsion from the college less of a major issue.

After this unhappy event Csokonai wrote only one more philosophical poem in the vein of his early reflective verse, his greatest: the one-thousand lines of "Halotti versek" ("Funeral Verses"), also called "A lélek halhatatlansága" ("The Immortality of the Soul"). The poem has a sad, indeed, tragic history. In 1804 Count Rhédey asked Csokonai to write an obituary poem for his wife's funeral. Such occasional poetry was in the Calvinistic tradition of the time, and students and preachers wrote hundreds of them. At the funeral in Nagyvárad (Oradea), the poet caught a bad cold that developed into pneumonia and actually led to his early death. It was this sudden sickness that prevented him from participating in the postfuneral activities, an absence the count took as a personal offense from a rude, uncourteous, and boorish poet. The poem was published at the count's request but without the poet's knowledge and in such a mutilated version that Csokonai's pride as an artist was severely hurt. Never before had he given in to fury as in the letter clarifying the situation to the count. It is a sad irony of fate that Csokonai, who longed all his life to see some of his works published, had to be hurt beyond repair by the publication of one of his major achievements. The letter to Rhédey is a heartbreaking disclosure of physical sufferings as well as the additional pain over his "stolen," "dismembered" work (II, 990).

The poem constitutes a summing up of some of his earlier ideas. However, it is different in tone. Csokonai was a different person by then; experience had matured his soul and toughened his mind. His youthful self-reliance gave way to a more sober attitude, to painful doubts, and to a Hamlet-like questioning. The brief prose introduction discusses the difficulty of finding a suitable subject for a funeral audience of people with various backgrounds. After careful pondering, he decides that the immortality of the soul, as an issue of universal human concern, might be a suitable theme. The way the theme is presented is a fine example of how to talk about sophisticated matters to a low-brow audience without oversimplifying and thus distorting the issue and without unconcern for people's understanding. The explanatory, storytelling style solved this problem most successfully. As most of the early philosophical poems, this one is also written in twelve-syllable couplets but the sentences are long; they cover four, sometimes even six to eight lines, thus producing a heavy flow corresponding to the weight of the topic. The poem is divided into seven parts. Csokonai took his motto from Rousseau. The statement that he did not try to argue or to convince, but simply wanted to expose his own feelings, served as a valid excuse to those who might have been offended by any part of the complex poem, and enabled Csokonai to present the whole stream of ideas as an example of his own personal anguish. Part 1, "Frightening and Cheerful Doubts," opens with Hamlet's question:

> To be or not to be—question of questions.
> The solution is hard, dubious, beautiful.
> A great question in which, searching,
> I find depth and wonders beyond the deep.
> The mind sees and wavers, the heart fears and yearns,
> and turning in my soul, the issue sighs.
> I feel my nobleness, I feel my weakness.

> My hope darkens and my doubt turns clear.
> And lifting this animated mud to heaven,
> I find no divine flame in body's dust.
> My ethereal wings take me to the stars,
> while my lead legs pull me to grave's edge.
> Indeed, I am hanging between heaven and earth.
> I am angel and beast, or mere dust and breath.

Pope's classically impersonal "man" becomes with Csokonai a most personal "I," turning the whole tormenting search into an individual experience. The topic is of commonly shared concern, but the solution to the problem is each man's lonely way. The poet feels engulfed and crowded by a series of questions, such as "If I have to pass away, why did I have to live?" or "Somebody doomed to perish why must he nurture Hope?" Thus tormented, Csokonai concludes with an almost existentialist description of the human existence:

> To be: a heaven amid a thousand temporal cares.
> Not to be: a hell we cannot fathom.
> Here I stand on an island of blooming life,
> on a cliff's tower high above the waves.
> Here I observe the shores' unmeasurable distance—
> my life's beginning or end.
> Below me the mouth of chaos roaring,
> snapping with the teeth of things.
> His magic left arm stretches toward me through yellow haze.
> "You die," he roars. I am terrified.

The picture is not all that dark, though, "under blue hope's curtain," encouragement approaches the poet's eternal soul.

Part 2, "Reasonings, Feelings," starts with a meditation on the destructiveness of death. It concludes with the idea that there is no total annihilation, only decomposition since each particle is accounted for. Annihilation could only come from God. The following passages address man's various images of God, the angry and the merciful. Csokonai tries to convince himself, that God, "wise," "good Father," and "just," could not destroy what He created in His own image. Unfortunately, unlike the world of nature, the moral world, that is, the human civilized world, gives little hope to the poet in his search for such a God:

> But let me enter the world of morality,
> and I don't know what to believe, feel, or do.

> Observing the actions of men,
> I find no good, wise, just God
> as I'd found in nature
> and before Whom I knelt with broken heart—
> virtue is worthless.

After a heartbreaking description of human injustices, the poet, almost mad with grief, asks for a devastating earthquake that would bury the thief, the meek, the murderer, and the murdered in one common grave, on which he would place this inscription: "Here lived plumeless two-legged animals." The animals, nature's children, nurtured by nature, fare better. Man comes naked into the world and immediately needs company, food, and clothing. Angry and indignant over God's cruelty for having thrust him into such unfavorable conditions, Csokonai decides to resign from the human state and to side with the animals. He hopes that Rousseau, that lover of the natural, would enjoy the sight of "an animal with soul." Imagination takes the poet into a short happy stay with animals when a storm suddenly disperses his companions and he is left alone, cold, and searching for fire. Fire reminds him of man. Once more he feels dignified being human, like a governor on earth for God. Compassion for his fellowmen overtakes him:

> Behold, while I was counting myself a man,
> I overlooked man's value,
> and now in that human species I'd discounted,
> four million men fill my heart.
> Lord! all are your creatures, all equal;
> I am only one of them, thinking, feeling together.
> Only some are advanced,
> the rest are still stupid—more or less—
> some are zealous, some are lazy; some passionate, some cool;
> rude, meek; sociable, rigid—
> yet on all their hearts they bear a seal
> that marks and guards their value as men.

They all feel "that death is not the final terminal." The conclusion reminds the reader once more of Pope, with "I can only be a man—no more, no less— / neither beast nor angel." The enlightened citizen of the world now tries to determine how people discovered this commonly shared truth; the immortality of the soul. In his probe into the question he is guided by the knowledge

that faith is an older road than reason:
Each nation becomes theological before
turning skeptical and full of philosophy.

Part 3, "People, Revelation without Philosophy," is about primitive people who "feel like beasts and think little." Part 4, "Philosophers," presents the other extreme, philosophy without revelation in the form of a personal visit to three dying men. The first visit is to Atheus who daringly denied the existence of a God whom he could not see. From Atheus the poet turns to the Chinese sage Confucius and puts the poem "Az álom" ("The Dream") into his mouth. This great lawmaker praised God but had no knowledge of the immortal soul. The third man visited, Socrates, with his belief in the immortal soul, symbolizes a higher stage of development. Part 5, "Christianity," that is, "Philosophy as well as Revelation," appears as the ultimate synthesis. Much of Pope's "The Dying Christian to his Soul," which Csokonai translated, went into this fifth part. However, the closing lines: "Thy sting, Oh death! show, / and thy victory, Oh coffin!" recall a well-known song of the Hungarian Reformed Church. The words are pronounced by the dying as he is being lifted up to heaven; the Eastern church song, celebrating Christ's resurrection and victory over the power of death, strikes a note of hope.

Part 6, "The Character of the Deceased Lady," has a self-explanatory title, while part 7 is "The Farewell Poem." Csokonai's great philosophical poem, similarly to other occasional funeral verses, ends with compliments to the deceased and to the audience.

II *Anacreontic Poetry*

Because of its ideology of mirth and cheerfulness, Anacreontic poetry has affinities with the bright optimistic outlook of the Enlightenment. Wine drinking, though, is not only associated with cheerful events but also with funeral feasts. Thus, the wine song may indicate gloomier moods as well. It is no surprise, then, that Csokonai presented what he called his "simple philosophy" in "Jegyzések és értekezések az Anakreoni dalokra" ("Notes and Essays on Anacreontic Songs").

In Anacreon's world—the poet says—the human spirit not only looks for the beautiful, the good, the delightful, but free of miserliness, ambition, useless worries: man feels that life is good and looks at death as that last stage of mirth and satisfaction which brings acquiescence. Horace followed Anacreon and gracefully admitted among his delights death, the coffin, and the other world. Let us live cheerfully, then, and with the least possible anguish, since we are going to die anyway; this is the philosophy of the ancient lyricist; if we have to live and be cheerful, let others live and be cheerful too, this is the philosophy of all mankind. I wish I could make the miser, the ambitious, the lecher accept this simple philosophy." (II, 206)

His own personal disasters made Csokonai cautious about the wonder-working power of the human reason. His resilience saved him from lapsing into total despair. So he put faith in this "simple philosophy," in a "live and let live" attitude, a hope that people would at least restrict themselves so that they do not hurt others.

In his proposed volume of Anacreontic poetry Csokonai planned to include as the last piece "A Hafíz sírhalma" ("The Grave of Hafíz"), a poem ranking with the best of his philosophical poems. Csokonai takes us to the Orient, to the grave of a Persian fellow poet. At this stage of his life, back in Debrecen, without money, without a job, without anything published, in order to satisfy his urge for mirth and oblivion Csokonai has to undertake a fantasy journey; he needs to escape the real world altogether. Only thus can he hope to enjoy the peaceful state provided by his simple philosophy, since others will not let him live cheerfully. Csokonai's concern for his nation's Asiatic origin makes us understand his interest in Hafíz. Géza Képes tracked down the poet's knowledge to a Latin work of the British orientalist, Sir William Jones, and to the Latin translation of the Persian poet by Count Charles Reviczky, a Hungarian nobleman and ambassador in London.[3] The loosening up of the usually heavy verse of reflective poetry into short lines suggests a more relaxed atmosphere. The refrain is sung by a choir of girls:

> Be blest, grave of Hafíz.
> There rests
> in the roots of roses
> the sweet singer of the Orient.

Indeed, the whole poem abounds in the smell of roses, and languishes into decadence; delight and love faint into an oblivion that is conducive to death. It is a poem in which life and death wish mingle inseparably and convey a kind of morbid peacefulness. The vocabulary of Hungarian folksongs, "Kökényszemű" (dark-blued eyed), merges with the lush atmosphere of distant Persia as this poet of

Debrecen, in the Hungarian capital of Puritanism, writes a poem set in a cemetary and in which the atmosphere seems to explode with hidden and overt eroticism. The very first stanza is indicative of the confusion; the grave indicates grief or at least the mourning tone of sentimental poetry, but the Oriental "brown ladies" as well as the "dark-blue-eyed" Hungarian peasant girls, dressed in silk, "with arms embracing" among roses and singing "tiny songs," remind the reader of a rococo readiness for lovemaking. The wine provides the longed-for oblivion. In this pleasant environment, the poet wallows in a carousel of scents, maidens, and flowers:

> The rose, a queen,
> sits on her brilliant throne
> and around her,
> narcissuses attend her court.
> Tulips, honeysuckle,
> and hyacints throw themselves
> before the royal throne.

(For the Hungarian flower *kökörcsin*, a Southern flower, "honeysuckle" has been substituted.) With the inevitable nightingale's song added to the lush scene, the background is complete. The description of the rococo bird's song displays unique linguistic virtuosity,

> Lulling, it drifts down,
> then climbs, adding filigre,
> and now it rings, and now grumbles—
> meanders, hurries, trills, extends.
> How strong and cheerful,
> how weak and how lovely!

The reader then is taken by surprise to learn that the poet longed for this voluptuous scenery only because this is the "sages' country" where "reason's altar stands." Among a superabundance of lush vegetation, an overflow of scents where a hundred poets sing and put wreaths on the grave of Hafíz, Csokonai feels that he has found an enlightened haven.

But the maidens of the Orient assemble there too. An unequivocally erotical description refers to eyes, arms, mouths, faces, bosoms, hearts. Nature itself joins in this ecstasy:

What do I feel? the flowers
peek from their buds,
their scent growing, bubbling.
And clouds scatter
for the mild sun
to smile through a clear sky,
The nightingales sing
and through the roses,
the breeze takes a stroll.

The appearance of young men turns the lamentation into a kind of
almost sacrilegious nuptial as the maiden greet them:

You curly, coppery young men,
who from the orange grove
now approach this grave,
hurry to us.
We are open to love; melt
our fervent hearts.

The poem illustrates Csokonai's defiant attitude. Determined to cling
to his simple philosophy, though grief-stricken, the poet manages to
survive by escaping into the fancied world of mirth. The imagined
world may be a distant century—the twentieth or the twenty-first of
his reflective poetry—or a geographically distant alien land with an
alien culture, as in "The Grave of Hafíz."

III   *Philosophical Message in Love Poetry*

Dante, Petrarch, the Metaphysicals, and many other poets chose
to deal with fundamental issues in love poetry. After his exile from
Debrecen, Csokonai followed this tradition when his grief over frustrated love added more intensity to his feelings of alienation. His
unfortunate experience with a girl—called Lilla in his poems—
caused Csokonai to meditate more deeply than before on the meaning or meaninglessness of life. His ability to unite thought and feeling
enabled him to create a love poetry rich in reflective meditation and,
at the same time, emotionally loaded, very personal, and sometimes
almost confessional.

A fine example of such poetry is "Újesztendei gondolatok" ("New

Year Thoughts"), written in 1798 when Csokonai was translating
Horace, which may have suggested the four-line stanzas with the
variation of iambic and trochaic feet, thus underlining the basic
structural device of contrasting elements, and also the swing of the
pendulum measuring out time. Csokonai's special rhymes make this
poem unique in the language. The oncoming New Year brings out
reflections about the passing of time. The central theme, time, is
examined on an astronomical, geological, human, and finally on a
personal level. Both the first part, with its scientific images, and the
second half, the real love poem, are reminiscent of Donne and
Marvell. The poem starts with a concise, pointed address to its true
hero, time:

> Oh time, racing time!
> Our years fly on eagle's wings
> and none return,
> all diving to the lap of Chaos.
>
> Oh time, you entity
> without beginning or end,
> only the temporal mind
> portions you into pieces.
>
> Did the world birth you
> or you the world?
> Without the tracking sun
> we would not be able to measure you.
>
> Perhaps because of you, Oh time,
> you who destroys all we have and are,
> even the sun is burning to coal.

Eternal change and continuous annihilation are first exemplified in
the region of the stars, and later in earth's geology:

> Many a vast plain is now an archipelago,
> valley's depth is mountain's peak,
> and where hill or grove once stood,
> bottomless salty seas began.

A series of illustrations from human history follows. Land turns into
sea, valley turns into mountain, arable land turns into civilized ter-
rain and back again, while

Today oxen plough the land
where Troy (the world's wonder) stood,
and where land was ploughed,
now London stands, the wonder of the world.

The thought of the disappearance of great nations reminds the poet of
the individual's even greater vulnerability in terms of time:

Oh, if in the great nations'
fates you show such power,
what about us little men?
What chance do we have?

In a chilly frisson the poet suddenly realizes the passing away of his
own life, and the inexorable, irreversible power of time over himself:

At least I am not a child now.
I've managed to survive four times six years,
and by doing so, of man's alloted time
I've used a third.

The closing part of the poem reminds of Marvell's "To his Coy
Mistress":

And since the days
sweep away even the sweetest times
while the young months
bloom, let us catch them.

The friendly spring? it flees;
the fog, in mourning, shrouds the velvet dawn;
the blooming hyacinth faints;
the rose welts in a single noon

while youth itself
abandons your graceful face.
Amor's bright star
burns out in your once winsome eyes.

Then, alas, your roses
won't be laughing from your tiny lips.
Then your sensitive heart
will be unable to rejoice or love.

And me? Only with thin
blood will I befriend my cold Lilla,
passing the days like a frigid,
senile pelican with sorrowful songs.

So Csokonai. Marvell puts it this way:

But at my back I always hear
Time's winged chariot hurrying near;
And yonder all before us lie
Deserts of vast eternity.
Thy beauty shall no more be found.
Nor, in thy marble vault shall sound
My echoing song.

In consequence, Marvell urges his coy mistress:

Now therefore, while the youthful hue
Sits on thy skin like morning dew,
Now let us sport while we may.

Csokonai has the same message:

Before that happens,
let us not Lilla, shun the vibrant time.
While life's fire rages
let us love. Let us share joy.

The similarity between the two poems is ultimately in the linking of
the idea of death with that of lovemaking and the awareness of the
inevitability of death. There is, however, a great difference. Marvell
uses the old device in a semiserious, almost playful manner to remind
his mistress that the passing of time leads to death. In Csokonai's
"New Year Thoughts" love is the secondary theme, appearing only in
the latter part of the poem. Time and death combine to dominate the
flow of ideas as the poet contemplates time's all devouring power with
dread and anguish.

In one of Csokonai's best-known poems, included in all anthologies, "A tihanyi ekhóhóz" ("To the Echo of Tihany"), the eight-line
stanzas in trochaic feet carry feelings of pain and mild indictment in a
balanced, controlled, dignified manner. The issues of the early reflective poetry reappear but the treatment this time is rather sentimental. The poet, hurt many times and in many ways, conveys his feelings

and thoughts to the Echo of Tihany on Lake Balaton in Western
Hungary. Finding no compassion in human society, Csokonai turns
to nature. The resounding echo, repeating at the end of each stanza a
series of laments, reaffirms nature's responsiveness. Now a mature
poet, Csokonai reopens the arsenal of enlightened ideas, but each
issue becomes a personal experience. Csokonai's most Rousseau-like
poem takes man-made evil: destructive laws as the key problem.
One such law separated him from Lilla, who had to marry a rich
merchant. The poem begins with a desperate appeal to the Echo:

> Oh, Tihany's sounding daughter!
> Emerge from your sacred wood.
> Behold, the one whom fate up to now has tossed
> is sitting on your shores
> in the pale moon light,
> bewailing his destroyed hope—
> a lonely, orphaned heart,
> a lonely, orphaned heart.

So far we have the perfect sentimental setting with all the conventional ingredients including moonlight and tears. Though the second
stanza introduces a real social issue, it is presented on the personal
level. Isolated and alienated from those who enjoy life across the
shore in Füred's fashionable resort, Csokonai finds companionship
only in nature:

> While those who know not grief and ruin
> revel in the arms of happiness,
> rejoicing at pleasant Füred's
> sources and shores,
> I am all in tears here. . . .

With the help of the Echo the poet hopes to awake Nature's compassion. In sharp contrast to the abundance of light images in his earlier
poetry, understanding nature appears now in a gloomier guise, recalling the romantic attitude:

> Dismal forests, rough peaks, crags
> resound my woes!
> Perhaps you sympathize more with me
> than do my fellowmen
> who cast me out of their hearts,
> who remember me with mocking and derision—

> a poor unfortunate fellow,
> a poor unfortunate fellow.

So says Csokonai in a bitter reference to his expulsion from the College of Debrecen. Indeed, in the next stanza the poet elaborates on this painful experience:

> My once good friends
> have spurned me now,
> have turned to the persecutors' camp.
> Oh, what have I left to feel,
> when they too eventually
> run at me as if I were an enemy
> though I have been faithful to them,
> though I have been faithful to them.

The feeling of being abandoned gains poignant expression in stanza five:

> There is none to comfort my soul—
> I have no comforting friends.
> He who hears of my fate shrugs his shoulders—
> all have abandoned me.
> Since there is no heart in men then,
> let me pour into your iron breast
> my heart's lament,
> my heart's lament.

As we have seen, the tears and the moon suggest an association with the then fashionable sentimental trend; however, the heartbreaking simplicity of genuine suffering raises this poem above the fad of the day. Indeed, it belongs with Csokonai's most mature writings. The ultimate blow to the poet, of course, was the loss of his sweetheart, but he refrains from blaming her at all. The loss is in no way attributed to Lilla's inconsistency, rather to society's cruel laws:

> Even Lilla who gave me hope,
> who was my only inspiration,
> Alas, Lilla took the tyrant's law
> and bowed to custom.
> (How are you now, blessed sprite?)
> I exist, abandoned
> in the ocean of anguish,
> in the ocean of anguish.

This grief-stricken, frustrated poet still identifies himself with the poet-sage of the Enlightenment, as in "The Grave of Hafíz," but this time Csokonai locates the hermit-sage in a dark, romantic setting:

> Oh, is there one more hermit dwelling—
> old cave, sacred roof—
> where a sage in silence and shelter
> may rest in these dark hills
> with only a stone for his pillow,
> where neither man nor bird comes
> to disturb me,
> to disturb me.

In the next stanza, this Hungarian poet, identifying himself with Rousseau retired to Ermonville, commits himself in his solitary escape to world citizenship. Unwilling to concede the defeat of his ideals, at least, for the present, Csokonai hopes to find them on the cliffs of Tihany.

> I think that I would
> not be breaking any law
> if with brave callousness
> I took my dwelling in among the rocks
> in the corner of this island.
> Like a Rousseau in Ermonville
> I would dwell a man, a citizen.
> I would dwell a man, a citizen.

As in "The grave of Hafíz," the escape into time is replaced here by an escape in terms of space. At this point of his life, Csokonai's most personal quarrel was with man-made laws that came to symbolize for him all injustices which he had tried to reveal in his reflective poetry. The decision to retire from the world and offend no law is a gentle but bitter satire on the evil law-ridden society he had to escape in order to achieve inner peace:

> Here in my natural state, learning
> to inspire my spirit
> from nature's reasoning,
> I would become wiser.

Once more the strange combination of Voltaire's problem-solving reason and Rousseau's natural state; indeed, where the two peacefully dwell together that should be an ideal world. Though Csokonai longed for it, "the unknown sacred solitude" does not seem to provide joy to the poet, who, still in a sentimental mood, confesses: "Crying I spend my days." He now intends to spend the rest of his life "in this dark forest" and hopes to be buried by "the neighboring peasant," a sign that his youthful criteria of literacy in judging people's worth was being replaced by Rousseau's requirement of compassion. At the end of the poem the future-oriented outlook of the Enlightenment prevails, and Csokonai finds solace in the thought of recognition after death:

> Then under the canopy of trees,
> my single grave
> would be blessed with my respected bones,
> would be blessed with my respected bones.

The illusion created by the reinforcing voice of the Echo leaves the reader with hope as the last impression.

IV *Darkening of Vision*

"A tihany ekhóhoz" ("To the Echo of Tihany") is really about the poet's unwilling withdrawal from human society, and so is the elegiac ode, "A magánossághoz" ("To Solitude"), written in the circle of understanding friends in Kisasszod after Lilla's marriage in 1798. The poet's yearning for solitude was not a momentary state of mind nor was it a result of the unhappy love affair alone. A letter to Bessenyei, soon after his expulsion from the college, already includes phrases reiterated later in the poem, like "nobody is with me and beside me only happy solitude." Csokonai considers books to be his only true friends who "are not evil like men" (II, 810). This, of course, is the very theme of "To Solitude." The poet's concern with solitude is proven by a later letter as well, written after his return to Debrecen, poor, sick, a failure: "Here buried in solitude I live for myself, for my country and for my usual studies, translating, reading, meditating; under my old thatched roof the envious do not find me; the bigot's misgivings do not reach me among my books" (II, 859).

It is nearly impossible to give an idea of the formal beauty of the ode in a foreign language. The eight-line stanzas consist of iambic feet which lend the poem a swinging tone as if the poet were carried away into a land of dream where the boundary between awareness and unawareness is blurred. Visual images and musical sound effects all combine to create a pleasant hazy atmosphere of unreality—a far cry from the clear-cut light images of the early philosophical poems. Similarly to "To the Echo of Tihany," "To Solitude" also owes much to Rousseau's philosophy, but a variety of diverse elements merge in this complex little masterpiece. Csokonai's landscape painting reaches its peak with the initial descriptive passage. As in his early reflective poetry, the stanza that carries the message, this time the indictment of social inequities, develops from the description. At the end, Csokonai emerges once more as the poet-sage. He never gave up the ideals of the Enlightenment, nor are his favorite rococo ingredients lacking, resulting in Poussin-like landscape touches with nymphs swinging between two hills by a lake or brook. The moon-light, with its nostalgic melancholy, makes the poem sound sen-timental, while the contrasting of city life to country life, with its negation of the former and affirmation of the latter, points to romantic affinities. The irresistible beauty of the poem relies heavily on the language; many of the terms and word combinations, Csokonai's own creations, are unique, they can be fully appreciated in Magyar only. It is interesting to notice that in this ode Csokonai dwells at length on the creative process. Solitude, sheltering, and harboring the poet from society's cruelties, releases his creative energy. In conse-quence, solitude is not merely an escape from society, it provides the poet with the peace and mirth he needs in order to give society his best: his artistic gift. The ode begins with an appeal to Solitude:

> Blest Solitude, come! cradle
> me with dreams.
> All others orphan me; do not abandon me too.
> Rock my spirit on your lap.
> I am sheltered in your dwelling. Such joy
> to have found you here in Kisasszod.
> It is good to dwell in this place,
> this place, the poet's delight.

The landscape comes alive with diverse elements, like "lonely dale," "freshening shade," "mossy roots of stumpy hornbeams," and nymphs, all responsible for making the place "the poet's delight." If the nymphs create a pastoral atmosphere, sentimental features add a new and different touch as in the most famous stanza of the poem:

> The areal moon pipes a soft light
> upon the leaves of the blond beach
> and sends a cool evening dream
> to the angel of the still night.
> Gentle Solitude! in such abodes
> there is sweet joy, delight for you.
> To your realm lead me often,
> There my weary soul finds comfort.

The social message enters in a strange, negative way. Those whom the poet blames for mankind's miseries—the kings, the misers—ask in vain for Solitude's solace; for Solitude despises them, shuns their company, and visits them with torments. Solitude's running from "teeming cities" and his feeling at home "with the feeling heart and gentle village and meadow" point to Rousseau's value system in which goodness is associated with the simple life. Solitude, then, appears as the epitome of that compassion, characteristic of the natural state, which according to Rousseau, was lost when reason won: "Those who this world despise / or whom it pesters," can trust sweet Solitude. Solitude grows in the poet's imagination into a strength-releasing power; the source of prowess, greatness and of the artist's creative energy:

> With you the poet strikes
> like swift lightning across a dark night
> when he creates new perspectives
> or out of nothing makes a new world.

The poet not only creates out of a void, but he also brings light into the darkness, because this sometimes sentimental, sometimes romantic Csokonai always returns to the ideal of his youthful days: the Enlightenment's sage and wise poet. In a confusion of stylistic trends, images of darkness keep on coming back with "nightly dew" and "death weaving its blind curtain." Solitude, a faithful friend, will accompany the poet to the grave. Death once more appears a brother to sleep. Overwhelmed by emotions and tears, Csokonai makes a last appeal to Solitude: "In your endless dreams I shall forget / this world's sufferings." The poem ends on a note of willful confusion. Is this already death's dream? Or is the poet referring to Solitude's comfort in life from life's evils through daydreaming—as he implied in the first stanza? At the end of the poem, Csokonai seems to be waiting for Solitude in death:

Blest Solitude, befriend me
when the grave will be my only property forever.
But when will that day come?
Blest Solitude, come.

A deliberate juxtaposition of dream and death scenes creates the
impression that Solitude's final blessing could only be reached in the
grave. Until then, when no escape into time or to a distant land is
available, Solitude's dreams provide the most efficient escape from
full awareness.

However, this withdrawal into solitude, an obvious indication of a
darkening of vision, cannot be taken as a sign of radical change in
Csokonai's outlook on life. Though "To the Echo of Tihany" and "To
Solitude" decidedly do not sound cheerful, they both radiate the
same humanistic ideals that inspired the teenaged Csokonai. That the
earlier enthusiastic voice became subdued is a logical consequence of
dark events in the nation's fate and the poet's personal life making the
bright light of the Enlightenment seem flickering and distant, indeed.

On his return to Debrecen, Csokonai precisely and appropriately
characterized the paradox of his own situation by describing himself
as "a cosmopolitan confined to a thatched house" (II, 868). Confined
he was in many senses of the word, and all his life. He was confined to
backward Hungary, confined to the position of almost a lackey imploring patronage wherever he could, confined to the role of "the
professional guest" all over Transdanubia, confined to his mother's
modest thatched house in Debrecen's Darabos Street, where a huge
closet served as the study of this most enlightened, knowledgeable,
and superbly trained mind. The discrepancy between his erudition,
his conscience of a world-citizen, and the thatched house illustrates
the extremes under which he was obliged to live. No one should be
surprised if such unbearable tensions pushed him to contradictory
attitudes. He was driven to more and more extreme positions by
misfortunes on the national and the personal level. His ideal was
represented by a statement which he had translated from Holbach:
"Be a man! Give the few gifts bestowed upon you by nature to others"
(II, 247). Expelled from the college and without a public forum, he
was prevented by circumstances from carrying out his ideals. He was
constrained to be that outcast he described in his farewell to the
Debrecen College students: "I have become a Timon, Gentlemen! a
misanthropical Timon, seeing that I am treated so much contrary to

humaneness!" (II, 795). Frustrated in all his expectations, including love, Holbach's advice became his only refuge. Holbach believed that, notwithstanding injustices, if you are acting out your life like a man "no earthly power can deprive you of that inner acquiescence which is the purest source of happiness." [4] As his physical refuge shrank more and more, as his thatched roof, ironically referred to in bitter self-irony as his "Sans Souci," burned down, it became more and more difficult even with the help of his simple philosophy to keep up the spirit of calm acquiescence. The confused images of darkness and death in some of his later poetry tell us of a deeply troubled soul desperately trying not to give up the ideals of the poet-sage. Though Csokonai continued his exercising in craftmanship, as in "A Nap innepe" ("The Sun's Festival"), celebrating the foremost symbol of the Enlightenment, these poems clearly do not reveal innermost feelings. On the other hand, three poems written to close Debrecen friends, in which Csokonai resorts to a more individual, almost confessional tone, tell us more about the poet's view of the world.

One of these friends, the physician and poet Dr. Földi, died in 1801. Nobody would expect cheerfulness in a poem written on such an occasion, but "Dr. Földi sírhalma felett" ("At Dr. Földi's Grave"), an antic ode, indicates the permanence of the poet's anguished state of mind. Csokonai achieves this impression by linking his own misfortunes to those of his friend and by making their frustrations part of the Hungarian predicament. In the first stanza "the acacias," the most characteristic trees of the Debrecen region, recreate the real environment. The very first word "unwept" may refer to the sad fact that the doctor's flirtatious wife was not present at his death. However, Csokonai reinforces the term "unwept" by adding "even You." The poet points out Földi's services to Hungary, thus suggesting a similarity between their misfortunes, and blaming the unconcern of the country at large for the sad fate of talented men. After five stanzas in the conventional pastoral tone, the poet strikes an individual note once more. Private and public concerns merge as Csokonai describes his personal grief over the friend's death as part of "the fatherland's commonly shared winter." Winter, of course, is a reference to the political situation. His praise of Földi in terms of the ideals of the Enlightenment, as citizen, friend, and scholar, turns sour because of the country's deafness to the poets' awakening voice. Csokonai's grief over Földi's death fuses with self-pity:

Yes, rest now great body: My country has ignored

128 MIHÁLY VITÉZ CSOKONAI

me too, though my precious blood
for her is shed, for her thinned, for her grows cold.

A comforting vision of the future appears in the last stanza, the vision
of "the human century" where "a faithful Hungarian's lute will sob"
over both their graves.

In the same year Csokonai started a second poem about his friend,
but never finished it. With its emotionally saturated intellectualism
and its almost dialoguelike conversational tone, "Dr. Földiről egy
töredék" ("A Fragment on Dr. Földi") sounds very modern. Földi,
presented as a man educated by "nature's investigator" Linnaeus and
"the master of good taste" Sulzer, symbolizes Csokonai's ideal of
knowledge combined with refinement; in twentieth-century terms
Földi can be said to illustrate the ideal combination of C. P. Snow's
two cultures. An angry Csokonai points out that the lute is hardly
enough to teach good taste in the Hungary of his time where the whip
could prove a more effective instrument. In the most interesting part
of the fragment, Linnaeus, initiating Földi into scientific research,
invites him to look into a telescope two ways. The first sight reveals
our planet's shockingly small size as compared to the immensity of the
universe:

See how small the earth is, half of it covered
with dark green water, half of it clear.
And like a half-ripe lemon swinging from its own
weight, hangs on the branch of great nothingness.

Wild bulls, whales, and elephants look like insects and "the proud
mortals" like ants. "In this perspective, all is piddling!" concludes
Linnaeus. Then he makes Földi turn the glass. Suddenly everything
becomes large. Beholding a dangerously menacing giant animal,
"You ask yourself, what is this Gargantuan thing—while from a girl's
hand / the tiny two-day old flee lunges away." The poem's most
modern line is a strikingly existentialist characterization of our
planet's position in the universe as "hang[ing] on the branch of great
nothingness." This is certainly not the vision of the poet of cheerful
disposition.

In 1804 Csokonai wrote a poem to his other Debrecen literary
friend, the author of the first Hungarian epic with a plebeian hero,
Ludas Matyi (*Matthias Gooseherd*). "Főhadnagy Fazekas úrhoz" ("To
First Lieutenant Mr. Fazekas") is a complex poem as far as fashions
and styles go. The beginning bears signs of the early attachment to

rococo with the appeal to "round dawn" to "hem the blue clouds," "link a coq" "to the tiny carriage," and then to go to the poet's friend, "to shine on him," "with a spell to take off dream's / poppy." But as soon as Csokonai speaks of going to Fazekas' garden himself, as soon as the situation becomes real, the style changes to the conversational. We almost see and hear our poet rush to his friend:

> Tell him . . . but never mind, I see
> he is here already, I see him.
> Behold my noble friend!
> See how he uses time—
> he whose name
> Bellona has glorified.
> Feverish haughtiness
> loathing, he turned to gardening.
> He shuns
> frentic enjoyment
> and watches, encouraged
> by a half developed flower.
>
> Coming upon bees (well-ordered society!)
> he lingers full of pleasure,
> aware that his fellow men
> handle the business of state differently.

Fazekas, noticing Csokonai, takes his pipe. Csokonai joins him:

> Come friend, let us loiter
> in the paths of your garden
> and laugh without grumbling
> over other people's happiness.

Serenity and calm satisfaction seem to characterize this friendship. The inner peace comes from a retreat to a Candide-like philosophy. With Fazekas this was his true life-style. The simple philosophy may have worked for him. The joking last lines seem to reveal sincere delight and cheerfulness:

> Come, let's kneel at this carrot.
> Come, see how this tulip lures us.
> Come, let us tip our hats to the pumpkin—
> all are useful, and sure, none does harm.

The final line, though, is ambiguous; carrots do not hurt but people

do. Csokonai was deeply hurt. His simple philosophy was nothing but
an escape, and serene acquiescence only second best in place of the
real thing, the public role as the nation's poet. Resignation rather
than cheerfulness characterizes the mature Csokonai. This gentle
bitterness should not surprise us, not after all the miseries of his short
life! In the 1802 Great Fire even his "Sans Souci," the thatched roof,
was destroyed. His mother's house became "A smoke-covered
home," as the poet put in the "A szélhez" ("To the Wind"). Indeed, it
was the wind that caused immense destruction by carrying the fire
rapidly over the city's thatched roofs: "How could I be cheerful?
Look, my Tibur is gone." And the bower of roses provides no shade
any more. Rococo's favorites: the roses and the rose garden are not
fictional this time; Csokonai mourns his own tiny garden attached to
the small house in Darabos Street. The loss of the garden and the
poet's grief are real. There is no pretense of cheerfulness nor is there
any search for escape. This time the poet bluntly faces cruel reality.

Csokonai's "ars poetica," his artistic credo, is often referred to as
the touchstone of his philosophy. His early statement in "A poétai
felvidúlás" ("The Poet's Cheering Up"), reveals the teenage poet's
preference of a cheerful Muse. "Grief fears me and sadness avoids, /
Even deep sorrow is cheerful around me," declares young Csokonai
in an attempt to persuade sorrow to give up trying "to endear" itself to
him. The sincerity of these lines is questionable. Many of his early
poems were written as school exercises in verse making and in the
practice of arguing for a given proposition. He could have probably
argued for sorrow as well; after all, Milton wrote both "L'Allegro" and
"Il Pensoroso." Indeed, at least one early poem sustains this argument. "Panaszkodik egy mindenbe szerencsétlen, de igazlelkű
ember" ("Lamentations of a Man unfortunate in everything but of
true heart") begins with "I almost despaired," and ends with "My
eyes are flooded with tears, / and grief descends on my head."

At different stages of his career Csokonai renewed his probe into
the poet's relationship to mirth and sorrow. Besides his personal
concern, conflicting European trends, such as the Enlightenment's
bright outlook and tear-loving sentimentalism justified such a search.
"A vidámtermészetűpoéta" ("The Poet of Cheerful Disposition"), an
exact contemporary of the great philosophical poems, contains an
almost ironical repudiation of the graveyard school of poetry.

> Place of horror! where the soul
> feeding on its fantasies
> walks trembling and frightened,

going back half-dead.
Terrible place! priding yourself
on your sad-lyred Young,
Farewell, mournful tent,
with your gloomy Englishman.

Such and more dark images are deliberately overdone in order to contrast with the pleasantness of Csokonai's favored pastoral:

I wish my annointed head
to be honored with a wreath
of bright color, gay,
heralding the fair sex—
made by the cheerful Muses
(soaring Graces)
whose pink fingers should weave it,
who bring it to life with ambrosia kisses.

The poet rejects even Racine and Shakespeare, the serious tragic Muse: to the sorrowful and sentimental he opposes a rococo Eden.

While the evening breeze swings
on wing through nectar-sweet
roses, little loves nestle
and prepare a heavenly harmony.

In 1803 he rewrote this poem as the introduction to his love poems under the title "Az én poézisom természete" ("The Nature of My Poetry"). There is no change in the message, but the form, the language are perfected with Csokonai's mature craftmanship. The first four iambic fainting stanzas with their enervated style suggest the atmosphere of the graveyard school of poetry.

Awful surroundings! where the soul
either flies on lead wings
or walks scared, fainting, growing cold,
then half-dead retreats.
Awful surroundings! have your Young
who is best at your grave;
"Farewell to you and your Englishman!
I am not English."

In stanza 5 Csokonai exposes the character of his own poetry. The trochaic feet are carried by a vigorous and sparkling rhythm that is almost folksonglike. However, the rococo atmosphere of "tiny roses," "little hyacinths," "softly ringing lute," "fresh evening breeze," and "tiny concerts" in the next stanza almost eliminates this impression of vitality. "The fainting song," no less indicative of a fad than are tears and graveyards, offers no real alternative to gloomy Young. This poem, with its preference of the rococo, was in keeping with Csokonai's early love poems. In consequence, the decision to include it in the love circle is not proof of cheerfulness. Indeed, the ambiguous note of decadence at the end warns against hasty conclusions. Moreover, other poems of his last years testify beyond doubt to Csokonai's darkening of vision.

"Az ember a poézis első tárgya" ("Man, the Foremost Theme of Poetry"), written in alcaic verse, a tribute to classical poetry and truly classical in its theme, reads like a summing-up of the poet's artistic career, and is also a personal confession about the way he sees man's place in the universe. The ultimate problems of human existence are back again, but they are not treated as a philosophical argument; the poet rather confesses his own feelings about them. In the first three stanzas the many-sided poet reviews the various fashions he tried out without refusing any or favoring any this time:

> Oh, thus far in what joys
> have my tender shooting days passed! Oh how
> I felt that life, and at Thalia's
> rose neck, lingering was sweet.

> With a shudder of ecstasy I walked
> the grand ruins where the Greek beauties
> walked, and streets of the Roman empire,
> and over their graves in sweet Italian gardens

> I picked the rare and succulent oranges.
> I beheld the French meadows; at Albion's
> caves and the German forests,
> in precipices I found joy.

The poet took to his lute whenever "new fancies" excited his soul. He describes himself singing in Dácia (a reference to the Debrecen region) and he seems to rise above the earth from his native city:

> I rose from the base of the earth.

> The cloud swallowed me, my heavenly fancies
> like waves, held me up, and I swam
> amid my thoughts, that ocean of wonder.

The stanza is reminiscent not only of Keats' "Ode to the Nightingale" but also in its wording of Dylan Thomas' lines about walking with his mother: "Through the parables / of sun light / And the legends of the green chapel." Indeed, no other poet in the English language is closer to Csokonai in enchanting musicality and the rich variety of imagery than the Welsh Thomas. Keats' poem ends in a sobering up; Csokonai returns to a cruel reality after being addressed by an angry voice as "the daring mortal, the animated mud," who, though "ungodly," dared "tread angelic premises." In a romantic rapture the poet forgot, for a short time at least, where he belonged, something the truly classical Pope would never have done. Annihilation is the punishment for this fatal forgetfulness: "Like a night star in areal haze / from the wide roof of heaven / falling fast to earth." Both "The Nature of My poetry" and "Man, the Foremost Theme of Poetry" were written after Csokonai's return to Debrecen. Evidently the latter is the one that speaks for the mature Csokonai, since the former is only a revision of a youthful poem. Though classical in theme and reminiscient of Pope's "The proper study of man is mankind," far from radiating the bright spirit and cheerful optimism of the Enlightenment the poem strikes a note of anguished despair.[5]

CHAPTER 6

Love Poetry

I Csokonai's Novel

A csókok: Egy történet az arany időből négy könyvben (Kisses: A Story from the Golden Age in Four Books) is a pastoral novel, contemporary with Csokonai's earliest love poems; it is the teenager's work which deserves to be ranked with poetry in view of the superb flexibility, beauty, and musicality of its language. Csokonai's remark, that poetry is possible without rhyme (II, 150), certainly applies to this little masterpiece, the peak of Hungarian rococo prose. The achievement is the more remarkable since Magyar prose was a poor vehicle for artistic expression at that time. The impact of Virgil, Tasso, Gessner, and Metastasio on the choice of the genre is obvious. The novel is a story of a social game, and young Csokonai was clearly enjoying playing with it. Though this early work attracted scant critical attention, it is in many ways the key to the better understanding of his love poetry.[1] The plot itself is simple, uncomplicated, and insignificant. Book 1 tells about Melitesz' despair over his frustrated love, his attempted suicide, and his rescue by the lovely tiny fairies, creatures of the poet's fantasy. In books 2 and 3, the hero relates the story of his love to the priest of Venus. He became acquainted with Rozália in the course of pastoral festivities, fell in love with her, kissed her in a kissing game in a maiden's disguise, and finally provoked her anger in a whispering game when he betrayed his identity. Book 4 is about the hero's search for his sweetheart and their happy reconciliation.

The importance of the novel lies not in the plot but in its way of presentation and in the underlying concept. Csokonai describes an innocent world, an Eden before the Fall.[2] There is no secrecy in lovemaking, no knowledge of evil, no sin in love. The priest of Venus, however, makes a prophecy about a fallen world, "a sad age," when "hearts will be bought with money, dresses, honors, and pretenses,

and not with the exchange of hearts" (II, 62). The tininess of Csokonai's wonder-working fairies is beyond all imagination even by rococo
standards. On the maiden's "forehead's plain amiable fairies gallop in
white rose carriages"; they also "sleep in her eyebrows' shady forest"
or else "in her face's pleasant meadow they weave their web of dawn's
chosen beams" (II, 60–61). Everything contributes to the "sweetest
harmony" in this paradise of "rose sponges," "tulip lamps," "rose
scents," "strengthening wine" and "honey taste." As in Csokonai's
rococo poetry, in the novel, too, sweetness is unseparable from
bitterness. Thus in the gentle world pain intrudes. Not only does
"scaring fear" seem to be "pleasant food for despair," but the pleasure
of love itself appears to have been a painful experience to Melitesz.
Kissing is not only sweet as honey but it also hurts like the bee's sting.
All this love-dominated Eden is "softly moaning." It comes as no
surprise to hear from the unhappy lover: "From Rozália's lips I suck
this death bordering on happiness" (II, 47). The thinking and feeling
that later produced the nuptial on the Oriental poet's grave is foreshadowed here. But while in *Kisses* all this is a game, in "The Grave of
Hafíz" the frustrated poet's despair is real.

The atmosphere and tone of the novel are in accordance with
rococo literature but, like most of Csokonai's work, it is eclectic.
Some enlightened philosophical ideas are hidden in this fairyland of
kisses. Nature and man, the pillars of Csokonai's reflective poetry,
are also ingredients of the pastoral. Csokonai calls himself "a singer of
nature's treasures," thus reminding the reader of Rousseau. As for his
protagonist he chose "a man" not "a hero" (II, 39). The tiny fairies are
not only protective of lovers, they also "accompany the sage," the
Enlightenment's ideal poet; furthermore, they are friends to the
poor: "They frequently fly over splendid castles in noble disgust in
order to visit with virtue, lying in dusk in the weed-covered hut" (II,
62). In their democratic sympathies and attitudes the fairies come
close to Rousseau's compassion. However, the rococo pastoral, associated with the French court and Madame Pompadour, clearly contradicts such ideals. Like his French and Italian models, Csokonai
created an impeccable bittersweet atmosphere of pretence in his
pastoral novel, but unlike his models, the Hungarian poet broke the
rules of ambiguity inherent in the genre when he overtly sided with
simple life. While the name Melitesz is in the pastoral tradition,
Rozália, especially in the form Rozi, sounds not only Magyar but also
folksy. Csokonai's digression from the convention, his introducing
folklife elements, is by no means an illogical extension of the genre,

and as we have pointed out earlier, Csokonai's rococo practice led to the emergence of folksonglike lyrics in Hungary.

In the beginning of book 4, when Rozi is found asleep, Csokonai unveils the whole rococo pretense in these words: "Be humiliated superb trees who are allowed into the pleasure gardens of kings and queens only after careful selection, because I will glorify this paradise of plebeian willows. You, created to chase away boredom from the powerful, you, who taken out of nature's lap are forced by the fiddling gardener's shears into a strange way of growing, you prey-trees! You are not worthy of my pen. The free willow, where Rozália slept, merits to be sung by my lute" (II, 64). This unexpected turn in the youthful poet's pastoral tells us more about his sympathies for the downtrodden than his often ambiguous political poetry. Significantly, too, the novel was written at a time when early dramas betrayed some contempt for the illiterate.

II Love Poems

Some of Csokonai's love poems rank with the most outstanding in Magyar. He was planning the publication of *Lilla, érzékeny dalok három könyvben (Lilla, Sentimental Songs in Three Books)* in 1802, but it was published only after his death. The poems there collected cover his entire career as a poet. Very few of them were actually written to Csokonai's great love, the Komárom girl Julianna Vajda whom he called Lilla in his poems. This favorite name in Italian pastoral indicates in itself the dominant character of much of those three books which include a wide range of poems from some in the purely rococo fashion to the late mature lyric in the genuine Csokonai style. According to the preface, the planning and organizing of the volume were the result of a highly conscious artistic attitude. The poems, Csokonai explains, were not written in the order presented, nor to the same person, and some not even to any person in particular, nor were they intended as parts in a poetical novel. The publication and immense success of Sándor Kisfaludy's verse novel, *Himfy szerelmei (Himfy's Loves)* in 1801 greatly disappointed Csokonai who was fighting a losing battle for the publication of his much worthier works. Proud and self-confident, the poet contrasts the immense variety of verse forms employed in his collection to the monotonous uniformity of Kisfaludy or even Petrarch. There are differences in content, too. Kisfaludy begins with plaintive love and concludes with happy love after his marriage to the beloved. In Csokonai's Lilla cycle the beginning and most of the sequence is pleasant while "the ending is irreparably sad" (II, 232). The late poems are not about frustrated love, but rather about disillusionment in general, in broad terms, affecting the whole life. The late love lyrics, including also poems like "To the Echo of Tihany" and "To Solitude," with specific philosophical connotations, are indicative of the poet's darkening vision.

Controversial issues abound in Csokonai's love lyrics. His former student and first biographer, Márton Domby, made an emphatic distinction in the *oeuvre* between spontaneous poems written under inspiration and those produced for other people's pleasure. Domby's distinction is between "being Csokonai" or "being simply a good poet." [3]

Csokonai wrote his early love poems in his student years. Biographers disagree about his first love's identity; perhaps the poems were written to two different girls, or possibly the poet was in love with love itself, as very often is the case with young people. Moreover, we cannot rule out the possibility, that just as he practiced description and moralistic poems as school exercises, so some of his early love poetry may be merely self-imposed exercises following those Italian models he agreed to study for the literary study group. The artificiality of the rococo conventions seems to exclude sincere feeling or emotional involvement, but this is not necessarily so. Again, one biographical factor cannot be overlooked. Debrecen—as earlier observed—was a town of little gardens and Csokonai's friend, Fazekas, was one of the founders of a famous botanical garden there. In consequence, flowers, an integral part of the pastoral, were no mere conventional devices to Csokonai but a familiar part of his everyday life. Furthermore, though dominant, the rococo was by no means the only trend in his early love poems. Those poems range from the rococo through the sentimental to the folksonglike. This variety indicates a conscious search to find his own style and to perfect it. Probably at this stage love was not really important to him; what mattered most of all was the ability to express it in various ways with perfect craftsmanship.

The search for craftsmanship, of course, derives from the classical drive for perfection. Morover, self-expression was not only not expected, but was even rejected as contrary to the ideals of self-restraint and self-discipline. Originality had a different meaning for that age that had so much veneration for the imitation of the ancients. Though his poems were never impeccably depersonalized, it was only after Csokonai had experienced deep personal disappointment that overflowing emotions disrupted literary conventions in his lyric. However, as time went on healing the wounds over the loss of Lilla, love became only a starting point for a beautifully controlled and balanced outpouring of emotions. In consequence, it is not easy to dissociate the spontaneous poems from the craftsmanlike ones; as a matter of fact, in many cases even a single poem would have both characteristics. Furthermore, Lilla, love, frustration all become secondary when Csokonai gets intoxicated by the voice and sound of his own musical poetry.

Nowhere else does his poetry attain the powerful musicality found in some love poems. Words lose their importance; poetry achieves that remarkable closeness to music we admire, for example, in Swinburne. The message, if any, is not anymore carried by words but, as in music, by sounds, as is often the case with Dylan Thomas. All this creates added difficulty in distinguishing between spontaneous and craftsmanlike poems. At the end of the nine-months courtship Csokonai wrote a farewell letter to Lilla. It was unquestionably inspired by genuine frustration, and yet the poet employs conventional rococo terminology: "Ah, sweet but transient hope, more transient than dawn or the early morning dew dried up by the sun's first beam in the bursting rosebud's lap." In the next sentence, however, Csokonai turns to a simple and more personal language: "How uncertain are all the events in man's life; the mortal heart does not know that its pleasantest joy is but a step on the way to bitterness! How often is the purest and most faithful love unhappy" (II, 833–34). Since this strange mixture of styles invades even his private letters, we may conclude that if there is a unique phenomenon who is more than a poet and who is "being Csokonai" as Domby has it, the strange and disturbing mixture, the embarrassing and confusing mixture of sincerity and artificiality may be one of his distinctive qualities.

The poet arranged the poems into three books. All late poems are included in book 3, which contains the masterpieces; all of them are about the irreversibly sad ending of his love venture. As the hope for happiness fades into nothingness, the poet says a final farewell to the hope he frequently glorified earlier. Many of these poems remind us of late nineteenth-century aestheticism and decadence. There is a kind of beautifully expressed "fin de siècle" morbid pleasure in pain and torment. The poet delights in beauty so much that suffering seems to matter less. Out of this transitory suffering, transitory because human life is transitory, something permanent has emerged: art. Ephemeral hope, happiness, and grief are all defeated by triumphant art. The novelist Zsigmond Móricz, a student of the College of Debrecen himself, perceptively remarked about Csokonai: "He wanted to set a monument not so much to his love as to the expression of that love in poetry." [4] The reader is almost reminded of Oscar Wilde's statement about life imitating art. Indeed, Júlia-Lilla is as much a symbol as she is real. As the local Debrecen gardens merged with rococo flower poetry, so the real girl becomes a convenience for artistic purposes. This conclusion, though, has to be qualified. At least seven or eight poems have to be set aside for genuine sincerity. [5] In them Csokonai comes close to modern confessional poetry.

The love poems cover an amazingly wide range, from the playful dalliance and flirtation of rococo, through the sentimental, to the shattering simplicity of frustrated hope. The cycle's title, "Sentimental Songs," indicates that sentimentalism was not a negligible factor, but then Csokonai may have used it in the sense of Sterne's *Sentimental Journey*, meaning an attitude congenial to emotions rather than reasoning. In the late masterpieces of sincere feeling, intoxication with music prevails, and the beauty of images and sound softens the poet's pain. At this point, then, the reader does not know what is more important to the poet: his frustration or the art that emerged from it.

The bulk of the poems to Julia date from 1797. Sometime in the spring or early summer of that year Csonkonai made her acquaintance in the house of the poetess, Mrs. Bédi, in Komárom. Only a few of these poems are truly personal, all of them sad. The others, like the pastoral novel, bear marks of the rococo and of the folksong. In "Az alvó Lilla felett" ("Over the Sleeping Lilla"), written in trochaic stanzas, Júlia appears in the conventional pastoral surrounding and asleep. She is the forest's "pretty nymph" with "milk-white bosom" and "marble heart." The stanza

> In her two closed eyelids
> are my life and death;
> in that quiet shadow
> Amor dreams and sleeps . . .

displays the lovely confusion of sleep and love, life and death, that so often permeates Csokonai's poetry. At his command, nature—"tiny flowers," "cool shadow," and "pure runlet"—will take care of the maid; "Light zephyr, embrace her bosom gently, / on her half-covered breast / flow like dawn's mild light." The poet himself guards

Lilla's sleep and awakening. Watching her may be the only peaceful moment for the lover. Lovemaking is painful. Indeed, in "Haljunk meg" ("Let us Die") the ecstasy of love shifts into a morbid death wish; in the end the two cannot be separated. From kissing, the lovers gently pass into dying in one another's arms, and find ultimate pleasure and happiness in death. Only in death are they united forever:

> During our lengthy kiss,
> I would gladly faint,
> and in this happy hour, from your mouth
> I'd suck sweet death.
>
> Come, oh come, let us die!
> My soul is already departing.
> No parting in death, my love,
> Hurry into my arms.

Being alive and being in love is painful to the rococo lover. This is the theme in the three iambic stanzas of "A Pillantó szemek" ("Glancing Eyes"). There is a sustained conceit: glances hurt because the eyes harbor tiny Amors armed with arrows. They besiege and conquer the poet's heart. In vain does he implore his mistress: "Do not torment me, Lilla, with another siege. / Do not spark such damaging glances / from your lightning eyes." "You see, do you not, the teeming / Amors as they swarm, buzz / around your dark blue eyes?" In the last stanza the pastoral lover's defeat is complete:

> One of them has lit your glance
> and has flown into the hidden fortress of my heart:
> there he has settled in.
> In my hope's main tower, he has unfurled a flag.
> His wee feet have already trampled everything.
> Listen! How he does rage in there!

Some of the 1797 poems are fresh and rhythmical. "Az esküvés" ("The Oath") consists of three stanzas of six lines each; the third and the sixth of seven syllables, the others of eight. The poem owes its charm to the mixture of sophisticated playfulness with simple freshness and that gentle tenderness peculiar to Csokonai's best love lyric. Confessing to be caught by Lilla's charm, the poet binds himself willingly to her in a solemn oath in the hope that she, too, in a matching oath, will bind her heart to him. The third stanza reemphasizes Csokonai's commitment:

> On your snow white hand I swear;
> on your rose lips, your fiery eyes—
> you will be my love.
> I swear never
> to seek another love;
> either Lilla or nothing.

Delicate tenderness is the striking quality in the lovely "A szamóca" ("The Wild Strawberry"). Scent, taste, and color combine to appeal in equally pleasant ways to mouth, eyes, and nose. The strawberry's uniqueness consists in its capacity to produce a variety of pleasures to our senses, thus surpassing honey, cherry, rose, fig, and other fruits or flowers that excell in one quality only. This is why the poet is reminded by the strawberry perfection of Lilla's lips:

> Sweet strawberry,
> to gods and
> goddesses,
> I would proudly serve you.
> If only you could talk
> or kiss now while ripe,
> you would be like
> my Lilla's sweet lips.

The time of cheerful hopefulness was short for Csokonai. Júlia's practical father distrusted the unknown, jobless, vagrant poet. While Csokonai, in desperate search for a decent job, was frequently away from Komárom, the father was busily trying to find a more promising suitor for his daughter. In "Búcsúvétel" ("Farewell"), a lyrical dialogue in trochaic feet, Csokonai relates his frequent good-byes. This time there is not the slightest sign of playfulness or joy in pain. When the poet kisses Lilla good-bye in the first stanza, there is no trace of ecstasy in the kiss; here we witness genuine sorrow at parting:

> How painful,
> my love!
> As I begin to be happy,
> I must leave.

When the maid implores him to stay, Csokonai blames their separation on fate's cruelty. Lilla, conceding that they now must share whatever life brings, joy or sorrow, pleads with her lover: "Stay with me, / share the cheerful days / and the bad." But in order to achieve their union, he has to leave on a job-hunting trip. So he replies:

> On this trip too because of you I go—
> A necessary leaving,
> since on the one track
> our two fates now move.
> Your eyes, then, should not be marred with tears,
> my love.

The dialogue turns into a little enacted drama, and the one-line stanzas express the urge and tension behind the lovingly charming parting words.

> *Vitéz.*   Please, until I to your lap return. . . .
> *Lilla.*   For me. . . . Nothing else of you I ask.
> *Vitéz.*   Darling, love me!
> *Lilla.*   Honey, don't forget me!
> *Both.*   Since my soul lives with you. Good-bye.

Another poem of that memorable year is "A fetete pecsét" ("The Black Seal"). The seven stanzas in trochaic feet display a remarkable variety in the length of the lines. There are two eight- and two seven-syllable lines but the wonder of verse writing are the two last lines in every stanza, a one and a half trochaic foot each. Those short lines play an important function: they draw attention to the emphatic last word. This significant term is then repeated as the first one in the next stanza. Folksongs frequently employ this device for establishing close structural link between the stanzas. The poet, opening Lilla's letter with trembling fingers, is enacting a dramatic scene. The black seal, a possible bad omen, may signify death—Lilla's or that of her love for Csokonai. Lilla is referred to as a rose, but there is no delight in pain or death. Death is frightening now:

> My sweetheart's seal of mourning!
> What do you pretend?
> What news for a frightened heart?
> Life? Death?
> Oh, heaven,
> I tremble.

"I tremble: perhaps my rose / is prey to a tortured heart." So begins the next stanza. It ends with the vision of Lilla as she is waiting in her grave for the poet to join her. The good news of her love is life-giving; it chases away death. In this poem, love and life belong together: "Lovely letter! / My heart is alive." If the last lines are playful, there is good reason for it, and under the real circumstances cheerfulness is natural:

> My heart lives! Forever I say
> good-bye to my anguish.
> Come, Júlia; away silly fears.
> She still loves me, as I her.
> She is mine.
> My fair Júlia.

In March 1798 it was all over. With Júlia Vajda married according to her prudent father's wishes, Csokonai's loneliness was complete. The poem "Még egyszer Lillához" ("Once More to Lilla"), born out of the first poignant torments of his utter disappointment, belongs among the great mature love poems. Starting with a note of confession of desolation, it remains shattering to the end in its dignified simplicity and in the tone of gentle tenderness to the girl who hurt him so deeply. The poet wishes her all happiness. The seven stanzas in iambic feet reveal heartbreakingly frustrated emotions. When Csokonai was cheerful, he preferred the gayer trochaic foot:

> Because of you I suffer.
> You have pilfered my heart;
> sweet tormentor.
> I grow faint, remembering you,
> and perhaps in such pain I am doomed
> to languish eternally.

Fainting and languishing are usual terms in rococo poetry, but they are very much in order in this particular poem and so are the images of the darkness of sentimentalism like "no sun," "fog overcasting" the poet's life, and "lean dusk." Tears are not false here; there is no ambiguity, just sincere pain:

> Deep in despair, your idolator cries,
> since far from you
> hope has come to nothing.

> Only a dread dream sits in his numb lap now.
> And often, surrounded by horrible visions,
> he screams, Lili! Lili!

Both waking and sleeping states bring nothing but despair in this world without hope:

> How terrible to live
> when hope is lost
> and one must live.
> Then he lives yet lacks a soul.
> My lungs, too, though I am alive,
> heave, having no soul.

No morbid death wish here! Death is realistically assessed as the inexorable end to human life and suffering, without fulfillment in hope. "In vain, my treasure, in vain! / Only in death's cold tent / will you embrace me."

Equally moving is "Siralom" ("Wailing"), written in a simplified version of an old Hungarian verse with two rhyming couplets in each of the eight stanzas. It is Csokonai's most folksonglike poem, stylized in the manner of popular songs with the poet enacting a role. But the frustrated lover's part came naturally to Csokonai at that time; hence the freshness. The first stanza could be mistaken for a genuine Hungarian folksong:

> Like a dove, I moan
> knowing no comfort
> without you. Alone,
> I wander in a dreary land.

Singing of loss, feeling as if "robbed of delight," came easily to him: "Grief and lament" are his share now that he has lost the one for whom he has cherished life. Sentimental ingredients are not out of place here; indeed, "the pale moon" "keeping vigil" with the poet contributes to the beauty of this touchingly simple poem.

In "Az estvéhez" ("To the Evening"), Csokonai reverts to the trochaic feet of his more joyous times. In consequence, the form seems to contradict the sorrowful content. Grief and lament, of course, were still with Csokonai in 1800, but the immediacy of being hurt had been soothed by time's healing effect. The poet does not record the experience of being hurt but rather the memory of it. This creates a certain objective distance between himself and his frustration. He seems to enjoy his own mastery as he turns woe and sorrow into delightful music. All five stanzas begin with an appeal to "gentle evening," the understanding companion. Gentleness is the feature that best characterizes this charming poem. A certain disturbing dalliance with grief prevails in the wording, but the impact of the poem depends less on words than on sounds. The wording is simple and almost void of Csokonai's usual virtuous images:

> Gentle evening! I beg you, witness
> my grief.
> Instead of tears, make my eyes shine
> with soothing dew.
> Gone are
> all my old tears,
> so overcome am I
> with suffering.
> No one to weep with me,
> no one to pity me,
> I struggle to the end
> of my pained life.

The feeling of pain is so overwhelming that the message seems to be that in such torment the poet's only solace is delight in expressing it and thus creating beauty.

Even though Csokonai turned sorrow into beauty, grief was nagging at his heart. "Az elszánt szerető" ("The Undaunted Lover"), written probably in the same year as "The Grave of Hafíz," is full of the very same death wish, but in a different, more personal guise. Genuine experience dominates more obviously. One must admire how many different guises Csokonai was able to adopt. The very shortness of the lines underlines a situation of tragic urgency excluding any dalliance.

> Now I am nothing
> and nothingness invites me.
> Be numb in me,
> smashed heart;
> better the worms
> infest me
> than those inner poisons
> eating me away.
> Why was I born?

Why did I love?
And why live?
Alas, run away from the fair ones
as from tigers,
meek soul.

The poet is evidently tired of life; once hope vanishes, life becomes unbearable. Csokonai, however, is unpredictable. Quite unexpectedly, at the end of the last stanza, he turns to the humorous mode of student verse. With a smart trick, the poet incites his sweetheart to follow him into death so that he can take revenge and kiss her unfaithful mouth. The closing lines most inharmonously contradict the touching despair of wishing to pass from the state of being into that of nonbeing. The ability to play on so many tunes sometimes lured Csokonai into deceitful traps, thus marring the impact of some of his poems.

The pain caused by personal disappointment crept into some of his occasional poetry. In 1802 Csokonai wrote "Gróf Erdődyné ő nagyságához" ("To her Excellency the Countess Erdődy"). It is a strange poem, indeed, since it concentrates on the death of Czindery, the lady's first husband. The first part is full of nightingales and roses—both typically rococo. Then the poem turns intimately personal, and from then on romantic images prevail, like "caves' dark stomach," "ruined castles," "dark night of wild woods." The second part reads like a confession about the poet's life in terms of his love for Lilla: "Then I was bewailing Lilla, / that beautiful, that good, /iwith whom I left my heart, / as eternal deposit." The poet bewailing Lilla's loss becomes a chased, hunted person: persecuted by cruel suffering, he journeys through almost all of Hungary. Under such circumstances, when hope only appears in order to leave him more disappointed, burdened with doubt, the poet becomes weaker and weaker physically—a reference to his deteriorating tubercular condition. Life, ready to abandon him, appears in this poem as "a frightened bird," preparing to fly away. In a sustained state of precarious health and frustrated state of mind, life is almost undistinguishable from death. Nature, though, is compassionate: "pale time" is sheding tears over the poet, and even Lake Balaton cries out in pain. Though still alive, Csokonai—sick—feels dead. The blurring of the borderline between life and death became a sad reality. What may have started as an imitation of a fashion turned into grim truth, thus making it again difficult to distinguish between the artificial and the genuine in Csokonai's poetry.

If in most poems Csokonai expressed his grief in terms of inner suffering, in "Az utolsó szerencsétlenség" ("The Last Misfortune"), the feeling of being hurt makes the poet physically sick—perhaps because of his declining health. The stanzas, built on the variation of eight- and seven-syllable lines, recall the rhythm and melody of Debrecen Calvinistic church songs and lend additional solemnity to the desperate statements:

> From marrow-drying fires,
> my head hums wedged and heavy
> because my feelings go rank.
> My heart beats, I choke.
> I can do nothing
> but feel and suffer.
> My soul and body are sick to death.
> Heaven, earth, my treasure, forgive.

Having passed from a short time of happiness into a prolonged period of pain, the poet feels ready to calmly greet approaching death. Death, however, is not the last stage. As if his parting soul took sight of some heavenly light, the poet beholds hope. Is it a dream? Is it real? We do not know. But it does not matter. What matters is the joyous image accompanying it:

> But what do you make me see in future's
> mirror, blue hope?
> Oh, year, dressed in roses,
> Oh, Fantasy from heaven,
> Oh, voices, melting the heart,
> Oh, torchlights of the altar—
> Oh life, love,
> do not toy so with me.

Hope is the poet's innermost experience, as intimate as grief. He sees hope as flirting with man generally and with him personally. Once more rococo dalliance turns into felt experience, and hope becomes Csokonai's personal ambiguous fairy, sometimes uplifting and then again hurting like the tiny Amor shooting arrows. Indeed, the peak of Csokonai's lyric is the poem "A reményhez" ("To Hope"), a masterpiece of images and sounds whose full beauty can only be suggested in translation.[6]

"To Hope" is the closing piece of the Lilla cycle. It is based on one stanza from an earlier poem, "Lilla még ingó kegyelmed" ("Lilla, Your Still Hesitating Mercy"):

> Ah, indeed, they ran away—
> My sweet days of yore,
> while grief and mourning have drained
> my youthful dreams.

"To Hope" is a poem about personal grief, but also one in which the poet's craftsmanship excels as never before, especially his ability to create music. The poem consists of four stanzas of sixteen lines of varying length. The formal effects are so carefully planned that even the rhyming pattern is deliberate to the minutest detail. Some of the cross rhymes sound cheerful, others sad, as the content requires. The trochaic feet, by constrasting the sadness over the loss of hope, create that atmosphere of paradox peculiar to Csokonai's poetry where the borderline between hope and grief, between life and death is blurred. The stanzas themselves display Csokonai's diverse moods; the first grief, the second a rococo shower of flowers, the third a grim reality where the garden is gone, and the fourth a classically harmonious, self-disciplined farewell to Hope with the poet fully composed and totally in control of his emotions. The poem has frequently been compared to Mozart's music. The short lines and intoxicating rhymes create an unmatched musical effect: the images follow each other in an uninterrupted rapid sequence increasing the nervous tension. In each couplet is a new image, contributing to the urgency without breaking up the poem into fragmented pieces; the flow of ideas, rhymes, and rhythm is smooth. "To Hope" illustrates better than any other poem the pleasant cheerful form which contradicts the gloomy message and helps in creating the illusion of a middle state between happiness and despair: indeed, the very atmosphere associated with hope. Also, each couplet carries an action and, since the lines are very short, an impression of crowded activity is created. Csokonai even watches his vowels: the more cheerful the passage, the higher the vowels in order to emphasize hope. The number of high vowels diminishes as hopefulness fades. Like everything else in the poem, high vowels, too, have an important function; they counterbalance the depressing message, which is not the loss of Lilla but the loss of hope in general. Hope is not linked with frustrated love but with life itself. This final version may be based on an earlier poem, probably written even before the acquaintance with Júlia Vajda. Some critics suggest[7] that the poet may have been commissioned to write words to a patriotic melody at a time close to the Martinovics executions and to his expulsion from the College of Debrecen. The insertion of Lilla's name was, then, a later idea. Even if this hypothesis is not true, Csokonai evidently chose "To Hope" as the last poem of his love cycle for its universal message, as a summing-up of his innumerable variations on the theme. The poem, as it stands, is about the ultimate sadness of human life expressed in a form so beautiful that it only hurts gently, softly, and in consequence, pain becomes bearable even without hope.

The first stanza is an address to Hope which had deceived the poet. He is no longer ignorant, but has become aware. Hope never means to fulfill its promises, it is just "toying." It is nothing more than a vision, false and blind:

> Toying with mortals,
> heavenly vision—
> godlike,
> capricious Hope,
> created for his own sake
> by the wretch
> to whom, as to a guardian angel
> he continuously pays homage.
> With your inducing smile you fed me false promises.
> (Whom do you smile at now?)
> Dubious pleasures—
> Why do you tantalize me even now?
> Leave me alone.
> You were the one who encouraged me,
> and I trusted your friendly words.
> Yet you deceived me.

The second stanza presents a wonderland of flowers created by Hope: the Eden of innocence and youth. The third destroys this Paradise, but most appropriately does so in terms of flowers: in stanza 2 "the planting of flowers," in 3 their "withering away." In stanza 2 brooks invigorate the trees, the poet himself cheers up amid spring's beautiful garden, "spiced with happiness." However, in the third stanza spring turns into "wintry grief." In the garden of his joy, says the poet:

> My thoughts each morning
> like the quick bee

flittered lightly
from rose to rose.
I missed only one thing
amid my joys,
so I asked for Lilla's heart
and heaven granted even that.

The icy winter takes all away, not only flowers and trees but Lilla as
well.

But alas, my fresh roses
withered away,
my life source—green trees—
died.
My spring, my joy
fell to a wintry sorrow.
My good, familiar world
went to dullards and fools.
Lilla? Could I have
kept only her, then
my litany would not have become
a dirge.
In her arms, this season
would still be warm
and pearlwreaths
still mine.

The last stanza suggests the poet's self-imposed equilibrium, a reconciliation to the loss of Paradise. This stanza is exquisitely balanced. First there are images of mourning in abundance:

Leave me, Hope!
Abandon me,
since this torture
is enough to seal my doom.
I know now doubt.
My youth has left me—
my soul looks to heaven,
my body sunk to earth.
For me the meadow is a desert.
All that was green is grey,
the copse sticks and weeds,
the sun has sunk.

Eden has not disappeared, but Csokonai no longer sees it. "For me the meadow is a desert" is the key line. Only the ignorant who still harbor hope are allowed to see the Garden. For those who know, night overcasts everything. After a poignant illustration of the state of experience where meadows, green, the garden of stanza 2 have no charm, the poet says a final farewell to Hope by recalling again its soft, gentle, soothing, comforting impact and thus almost dispelling the mourning gloom of the stanza's first part.

> Enchanting, soft trills,
> colorful life,
> pleasures, hopes, Lillas
> Farewell!

The plural in hopes and Lillas is significant. Unlike an earlier personal farewell poem to Júlia, this is not a good-bye to any one person, but to everything in life that encourages Hope. The last farewell lines with trills, colors, and pleasures imply cheerfulness, though there is increased tension in the nervous beat of those short lines, which throughout the poem convey anguish and agony. But this is an anguish softened by beauty. Beauty that is fragile by nature breaks if handled carelessly. By implication, then, the poet's composure is fragile too; any unwanted intrusion of uncontrolled emotions would destroy it. The poem, an epitome to Csokonai's *oeuvre*, is about his fragile inner peace, relying on his simple philosophy, an easing of tension by singing. It is about the only escape he really cherished: artistic creation.

CHAPTER 7

Conclusion

A T the end of this issue-oriented analysis, three problems of importance should be reemphasized: Csokonai's political convictions, his alleged escape from reality, and his eclecticism. Ever since the great literary dictator, Ferenc Kazinczy, referred disappointingly to some poems Csokonai wrote after the disclosure of the Martinovics conspiracy, the poet's political views have been a constant topic of critical controversy. Kazinczy's misgivings are understandable, because he himself was imprisoned for several years for his association with Martinovics. In recent years, some critics have overemphasized Csokonai's radicalism in his early Debrecen years as well as his opposition after 1795 to the French Revolution. In trying to reassess the poet's attitude, I have come to the conclusion that at all stages of his life Csokonai was much more a patriot, a poet of the nation, than a political radical, and at no period of his life was he a revolutionary. It has also become evident that Csokonai, hard pressed by personal and national misfortunes, had to learn to live with the status quo. The necessity to live with, and the ability to survive, an unpleasant circumstance has been the Hungarian predicament throughout the centuries. For trying to serve the nation under any conditions, Csokonai should not be judged harshly; for making sometimes extreme compromises, he should not be condemned. In his resilience, in his practicing the sad art of coexisting with a frustrating political situation, he has set a model for generations to come.

Not only was Csokonai not a radical revolutionary in his student years; he was not an unqualified optimist either. What he himself called a "noble disgust," disturbs the enthusiastic tone of his philosophical poems that propagate enlightened ideas. On the other hand, even at the end of his life, in his frustrated and disillusioned retreat from the world, he did not give up hope entirely in what he described as a future "human century." Related to the issue of optimism and pessimism is the question whether much of the best in Csokonai's poetry should be regarded as an escape from reality. One of the poet's best critics, János Horváth, believes so.[1] Csokonai's own insistence on his "simple philosophy" may, indeed, justify such an assessment. Before reaching any conclusion, at least two points merit serious consideration.

By inclination, Csokonai preferred quiet, peacefulness, and pleasantness. Though nurtured on the cult of reason, and not shunning company, Csokonai felt a close kinship with Rousseau's attitude. In a letter to Count Festetich in 1798, he referred to what he called "my quietness-loving soul and my gracious little Muse" (II, 830). Many events of his life become clear in this context: his continuous search for a small property of his own where he could work in an environment congenial with his nature, even his application to the emperor to this effect. Csokonai's love for the rococo can be appreciated more fully in view of his search for pleasantness. Antal Szerb interpreted the rococo pretense of beauty as a kind of heroic sacrifice defying ugly reality.[2] There is no better proof of this than Csokonai's letter to Count Széchenyi, describing his little home after the Great Fire: "The roses were blooming when the blazing flames swept through my tiny garden and my Sans Souci . . . when the rose-grove burned down and the nightingale that used to give concerts each night, ran away mad" (II, 908). Indeed, what heroism went into this description of the disaster in rococo terms, into describing a thatched house in terms of Versailles, into keeping up a brave attempt to save at least the pretense of quiet and pleasantness! Since the real world around him was unpleasant and even hostile most of the time, the poet desperately tried to create in his poetry the atmosphere he needed for survival. While a student at the College of Debrecen, Csokonai was a very sociable person. He may have cherished his privacy for study and creative activity, but he balanced it by wholeheartedly participating in revelry. His later withdrawal from society was not voluntary, but rather a bitter necessity.

Besides his own disposition, then, a second, more important factor must be considered in this context. Adverse circumstances, starting with his expulsion from the college, made it imperative for Csokonai to create himself in his poetry a world where beauty and pleasantness survived. It is after that woeful event that the poet made his first reference to retreating into himself. Several letters of that period underline this argument. To Sándor Bessenyei he wrote: "And I am exiled in my country—I am happy only if I can find a new world for myself, there building a republic, a Philadelphia . . . and like Franklin, at least, there . . . *eripio fulmen coelo sceptrumque tyrannis*" (II, 809). The reference to the young American Republic and to Franklin make it very clear that the poet favored a public role and that he intended to act like Franklin, by actively contributing to his nation's future. The same idea is sustained in a letter to Gergely Berzeviczy, where Csokonai explained that "a poet and a philosopher—isolate themselves from the world and fancy to live two or three centuries ahead of their time." Here again he emphasizes the didactic role of poetry rather than an ivory-tower attitude. In the same letter Csokonai continues: "In consequence, the poet lives free in his imagined world, built by his own fancy, and the philosopher lives peacefully in his republic he has founded Plato-like according to his own imagination with his own ideas, where he is *sibi consul et senatus*" (II, 811). If Csokonai seems to support the idea of the poet's independence from the public world, such a position was forced on him by circumstances. But in their forced retreat from the world, as he sees it, poet and philosopher remain concerned with, and committed to, the problems of mankind; they contribute to mankind's progress through their writings which show the way to a better future. To the end of his life Csokonai was ready to go out into the world and to serve his country. This was what he really wished and hoped to do all his life. Hungary was not mature enough to appreciate Csokonai's superb qualifications and readiness for public service, nor was the political situation favorable. Csokonai's suggestion that he become the editor of a Hungarian paper published in Vienna makes it obvious how strongly he desired to serve: "it is not enough in the negative way not to damage one's country; rather it is our duty to contribute positively to its ornament" (II, 864). It was the tragedy of his life that Hungary did not require his service, though he offered it in so many different ways: as a poet, a teacher, a librarian, a journalist, a dramatist; in both the humanities and the sciences. He was even ready to go to Switzerland in order to study the dairy industry there and come back to teach at an agricultural college. He was truly interested in all those various fields from botany to poetry, was as well versed in music as he was qualified to collect dialect words and folksongs. What better sign of Hungary's unfortunate situation could there be than the fact that a talent of so diverse abilities—in order to preserve his sanity—had to pretend to prefer seclusion to what he really liked, public service, combined with facilities for privacy?

Finally, a word about Csokonai's way of writing. He started out in his great philosophical poems as a propagator of the ideas of the Enlightenment. His poetry, though never completely depersonalized, centered on the universally human, and treated issues in an objective, logical, rational manner. Csokonai's serious classicism was as well-balanced and well-proportioned as his elegant, refined, playful rococo. Many of his later poems benefited from that balanced harmony. However, very early the disruptive, asymmetric, unbalancing nature of mannerism added a shockingly different note to his writings. This tendency intensified after his exile from Debrecen. The more down-to-earth approach of folk art and of sometimes vulgar student literature strangely contradicted the pastoral, but in a way also complemented it, leading to a ruthless honesty in the observation and presentation of reality in some of the mature poems. Frustrating personal experiences weakened the poet's belief in the absolute rationality of the universe, and his own painfully experienced alienation made him more and more inward looking. His poetry became less an objective presentation of a seemingly rational external world than a very personal expression of an ambiguous universe.

Csokonai is almost unique in world literature inasmuch as his tragically brief career illustrates the development of European thought and artistic techniques from the optimistic belief of the Enlightenment in a rational universe where everything is for the best, to the hallucinations and visions of the tortured individual about an increasingly cruel and irrational world. Such a development was matched by a combination of styles starting with mannerism and pointing ultimately in the direction of twentieth-century confessional lyric.

No wonder Csokonai's influence on Hungarian literature was so overwhelming: the most different periods and poets of the most different aspirations found their model in him. The great romantic epic of the early nineteenth century (by Mihály Vörösmarty) owes him as much as the down-to-earth honesty of János Arany's descriptive poetry, and the natural, spontaneous simplicity of Sándor Petőfi's love poems in mid-century, or the Hungarian folk drama of the second half of the nineteenth century. In the early years of the present century, Endre Ady, Árpád Tóth, Zsigmond Móricz, incidentally all former students at the College of Debrecen or natives of Debrecen, all members of the so-called circle of *Nyugat* (*West*), striving for a rejuvenation of Magyar literature in line with Western models, rediscovered Csokonai's art, his smooth and successful assimilation of various styles, his word-coining and formal mastery, as well as his distinctly personal tone. The Hungarian ear discerns the echo of the eighteenth-century poet in many famous lines in Magyar lyrics. The language barrier constitutes such an obstacle that a single example only will be presented here, one that should also demonstrate Csokonai's striking modernity. In one of his late poems, in an existentialist image, Csokonai has earth sit "on the branch of great nothingness." In the twentieth century, Attila József borrowed this strange image and made it a symbol of modern man's utter loneliness and insecurity when he said in "Reménytelenül" ("Without Hope"): "My heart sits on the branch of nothingness." There seems to be a direct connection between Csokonai's "farewell" to Hope and József's poem, with Csokonai anticipating modern man's anguish, alienation, and frustration.

Notes and References

All citations from primary sources are included in my text followed by appropriate volume and page numbers, and all refer to *Csokonai Vitéz Mihály minden munkája*, 2 vols. (1973). (Place of publication is Budapest unless otherwise indicated. All quotations from Csokonai's prose works are in my own translation.)

Chapter One

1. For the brief historical account in this chapter as well as in chapter 4, I am indebted to the following: E. J. Hobsbawm, *The Age of Revolution 1789–1848* (New York, 1962), pp. 22–163; Béla K. Király, *Hungary in the Late Eighteenth Century* (New York, 1969), pp. 129–234; Henry Marczali, *Hungary in the Eighteenth Century* (New York, 1971), pp. 1–195; Kálmán Benda, ed., *A magyar jakobinusok iratai: Naplók, följegyzések, röpiratok*, 3 vols. (1952–1957); Denis Silagi, *Jakobiner in der Habsburger Monarchie: Ein Beitrag zur Geschichte des aufgeklärten Absolutismus* (Vienna, 1962).

2. Robert Townson, *Travels in Hungary with a strict account of Vienna in the Year 1793* (London, 1797), pp. 227–29.

3. For Csokonai's biography, I am most indebted to the following: Márton Domby, *Csokonai Vitéz Mihály élete* (1955); Viktor Julow, *Csokonai Vitéz Mihály* (1975); Géza Juhász, *Csokonai tanulmányok* (1977); Ervin Sinkó, *Csokonai életműve* (Novi Sad, 1965); Balázs Vargha, *Csokonai Vitéz Mihály* (1974); Balázs Vargha, ed., *Csokonai emlékek* (1960).

4. Márton Domby, p. 11.

5. Endre Ady, "Csokonai Vitéz Mihály," *Költészet és forradalom* (1969), p. 84.

6. György Poszler, *Szerb Antal* (1973), p. 236.

7. For this simplified account about Debrecen and the College of Debrecen, I am most indebted, besides my personal experience of several decades in that city, to the following: István Balogh, *A cívisek világa*. *Debrecen néprajza* (1973); Gábor Mocsár, *Szellem és századok*. *Betekintés Debrecen múltjába* (Debrecen, 1962); Antal Papp, *Debrecen*, 2 vols. (n.d.); István Szűcs, *Szabad Királyi Debrecen város története* (Debrecen, 1872); Dr. Sándor Nagy, *A debreceni református kollégium* (Hajduhadház, 1933).

8. Townson, p. 238.

9. For the data on Hungarian cities and the College of Debrecen, I am

157

158   MIHÁLY VITÉZ CSOKONAI

indebted to Martin Schwartner, *Statistik des Königreichs Ungarn* (Pest, 1798), pp. 112–13, 549.
10. *Csokonai emlékek*, p. 293.
11. All documents about the suit are included in *Csokonai emlékek*.
12. Quoted by Sándor Eckhardt, A *francia forradalom eszméi Magyarországon* (1924), p. 68.
13. Ibid., pp. 105–06.
14. *Csokonai emlékek*, pp. 38–70.
15. Quoted from an informer's letter by Benda, I, 483–84.
16. Townson, p. 239.

Chapter Two

1. Arnold Hauser, *The Social History of Art* (New York, Vintage ed. First American ed., 1951,), III, 140.
2. János Horváth, *Csokonai. Csokonai költő barátai* (1936), p. 51. For the most detailed account on the relationship between the school exercises and major poems, see József Szauder, *Az estve és Az álom* (1970); for Csokonai's eclecticism, see Viktor Julow, "Csokonai klasszicizmusa és manierizmusa," *Alföld*, 24, no. ll (1973), 71–84. For the treatment of styles, I am indebted to Arnold Hauser's work.
3. Mario Praz, *On Neoclassicism*, trans. Angus Davidson (Evanston, 1969), p. 78.
4. Arnold Hauser, III, 17.
5. Pál Pándi, "Jegyzetek Csokonai Vitéz Mihályról," *Csillag*, 4, no. 2 (1951), 219.
6. Helmut Hatzfeld, *The Rococo: Eroticism, Wit and Elegance in European Literature* (New York, 1972), p. 5.
7. Ibid., p. 93.
8. Viktor Julow, the first to deal with mannerism in Csokonai's poetry, considers only the continental scene and does not refer to the English equivalent, Metaphysical poetry.
9. Mario Praz, *The Flaming Heart* (Garden City, N.Y., 1958), pp. 253–54.
10. T. S. Eliot, *Selected Prose*, ed. Frank Kermode (New York, 1975), p. 164.
11. Arnold Hauser, II, p. 103.
12. Ibid., p. 106.
13. Ibid., p. 100.
14. Ibid., p. 128.
15. J. C. Smith, "On Metaphysical Poetry," *Scrutiny*, December, 1933, 234.
16. László Németh, *Az én katedrám* (1969), p. 207.
17. Sándor Domanovszky, *Magyar művelődéstörténet* (n.d.), IV, 625.

18. See Viktor Julow, *Csokonai Vitéz Mihály*, p. 121; Klára Bárczy, "Popular Tendency in the Works of Csokonai and Burns," *Hungarian Studies in English*, 9 (1975), 103–117. On this topic I am most indebted to Thomas Crawford, ed., *Love Labour and Liberty: the eighteenth-century Scottish lyric* (Carcanet Press Limited, 1976).

19. *Love, Labour and Liberty*, p. 6.

20. Ibid., p. 126.

21. Viktor Julow, p. 91.

22. Zsigmond Móricz, *Válogatott tanulmányai* (1952), p. 73.

23. Ferenc Kazinczy, *Összes művei: Levelezés* (1890–1911), XV, 518–19.

24. Csokonai's "purely" baroque poems are few and not significant enough to necessitate special discussion in a short monograph; however, the remarkable recurrences of unconventionally used baroque elements in his later poems justify the discussion of their contribution to the modernization of Csokonai's art.

25. Arnold Hauser, II, p. 174.

26. Ibid., III, p. 183.

27. Antal Szerb, *Magyar irodalomtörténet* (1972), p. 259.

28. Arnold Hauser, II, pp. 180–82.

29. Julow Viktor, "Csokonai stílusszintézise," *Árkádia körül* (1975), p. 177.

Chapter Three

1. László Németh, p. 213.

2. Balázs Vargha, ed., "Csokonai Vitéz Mihály nemzetközi Helikonja," *Arron*, 9 (1976), 168–75.

3. See Dezső Baróti, *Irók, érzések stilusok* (1971), pp. 204–40; Viktor Julow, *Csokonai Vitéz Mihály*, pp. 176–89; Ervin Sinkó, pp. 178–98. I am most indebted to Sinkó's imaginative approach.

4. Viktor Julow, "Pope *Fürtrablásának* ismeretlen magyar fordítása," *Árkádia körül*, pp. 194–205.

5. For the most detailed analysis, see Pukánszkyné, Jolán Kádár, *A drámaíró Csokonai* (1956); on the baroque character of his plays, see p. 6.

6. See Sinkó, p. 79.

Chapter Four

1. Julow Viktor, "Talányos Csokonai—tragikus Csokonai," *Árkádia körül*, p. 128.

2. Géza Juhász, "Csokonai 'Forradalmi Katé'-ja," *Csokonai tanulmányok*, pp. 200–207.

3. A. de Gérando, *De L'esprit public en Hongrie depuis la Révolution Française* (Paris, 1848), p. 50.

4. Viktor Julow, *Csokonai Vitéz Mihály*, p. 133, condones the College's act as an act of self-defense and even as a possible protection for Csokonai against political charges, while Sinkó (pp. 18–21) discusses it in terms of cruelty to the young poet.

5. See Viktor Julow, p. 8.

6. E. J. Hobsbawm, p. 32.

7. The most consistent advocates of the radical Csokonai image are Géza Juhász, Pál Pándi, and Imre Waldapfel.

Chapter Five

1. J. J. Rousseau, "Discourse on the Origin and Foundation of the Inequality of Mankind," trans. Lowell Bair, in *The Essential Rousseau* (New York, 1974), p. 173.

2. Géza Juhász, *Csokonai tanulmányok*, p. 211.

3. Géza Képes, "Hafiz et Csokonai," in *Littérature Hongroise—Littérature Européenne* (1964), pp. 287–303.

4. My English translation is based on Csokonai's Magyar.

5. I disagree on this point with Viktor Julow, p. 79.

Chapter Six

1. János Horváth, p. 41.

2. Ervin Sinkó, pp. 57–66.

3. Márton Domby, p. 60.

4. Zsigmond Móricz, p. 71.

5. János Horváth, p. 47.

6. Among the innumerable interpretations of this poem, the best is by Tamás Kiss in *A lírai mű megközelítése* (1969), pp. 29–39.

7. Géza Juhász, pp. 355–61; Balázs Vargha, *Csokonai Vitéz Mihály alkotásai és vallomásai tükrében*, pp. 89–95.

Chapter Seven

1. János Horváth, p. 25.

2. Antal Szerb, p. 259.

Selected Bibliography

PRIMARY SOURCES

1. Collected Editions

Csokonai Vitéz Mihály poétai munkái. Edited by József Márton. 4 vols. Bécs: Pichler Antal, 1813.
Csokonai Vitéz Mihály minden munkái. Edited by Ferenc Schedel. Pest: Hartleben, 1844.
Csokonai Vitéz Mihály összes művei. Edited by István Harsányi and József Gulyás. 3 vols. Budapest: Genius, 1922.
Csokonai Vitéz Mihály összes művei. Budapest: Franklin, 1942.
Csokonai Vitéz Mihály válogatott művei. 2 vols. Budapest: Szépirodalmi Kiadó, 1950.
Csokonai Vitéz Mihály elegyes poétai munkái mellyeket mint debretzeni deák irt, (1789–1795). Edited by Géza Juhász. Debrecen: Alföldi Könyvnyomtató, 1955.
Csokonai Vitéz Mihály összes versei. Edited by Balázs Vargha. 2 vols. Budapest: Szépirodalmi Kiadó, 1956.
Csokonai Vitéz Mihály minden munkája. Edited by Balázs Vargha. 2 vols. Budapest: Szépirodalmi Kiadó, 1973.

2. Individual Editions

A szépség ereje a bajnoki szíven. Debrecen, 1800.
A tavasz. Irta Kleist. Komárom, 1802. A translation.
Dorottya. Nagyvárad: Gottlieb, 1804.
Halotti versek. Nagyvárad: Gottlieb, 1804.
Alkalmatosságra írt versek. Nagyvárad: Gottlieb (?), 1805.
Lilla. Érzékeny dalok három könyvben. Nagyvárad: Gottlieb, 1805.
Ódák. Nagyvárad: Gottlieb, 1805.
Anakreoni dalok, Bécs: Pichler, 1806.

3. English Translations

"To Hope." In *The Magyar Muse*. Edited and translated by Watson Kirkconnel. Winnepeg: Magyarujság press 1933. Also in *Hungarian Authors*,

translated by Joseph Grosz and W. Arthur Boggs, (Münich: Griff, 1963);
100 Hungarian Poems, edited by Thomas Kabdebo, translated by Watson Kirkconnel, (Manchester: Albion Editions, 1976).
"The Strawberry," "To Bacchus," and "To My Friend." In *Poetry of the Magyars*. Edited by John Bowring. London: R. Heward, 1830.
"Shy Request." Translated by Ina Roberts; "Susie's Lament for Johnny," translated by Anthony Edkins; "To Solitude," translated by Edmund Blunden. In *100 Hungarian Poems*.

SECONDARY SOURCES

1. Books

BÉCSY, TAMÁS. *A drámaelmélet és dramaturgia Csokonai műveiben*.
    Budapest: Akadémiai Kiadó, 1978. A study of theory and techniques in
    Csokonai's dramas.
DOMBY, MÁRTON. *Csokonai Vitéz Mihály élete*. Pest, Trattner János, 1817;
    also Budapest: Magvető, 1955. The first biography on Csokonai, written
    by a former student of his at the College of Debrecen.
ELEK, ISTVÁN. *Csokonai versművészete*. Budapest: Királyi Magyar Egyetemi
    Nyomda, 1941. The only detailed analytical study of his verse forms.
FERENCZI, ZOLTÁN. *Csokonai*. Budapest: Franklin, 1907. The first
    twentieth-century analysis.
HARASZTI, GYULA. *Csokonai Vitéz Mihály*. Budapest: Aigner, 1880. The best
    nineteenth-century monograph; biography and criticism.
HORVÁTH, JÁNOS. *Csokonai: Csokonai költő-barátai: Földi és Fazekas*.
    Budapest: Kókai Lajos, 1936. A remarkably perceptive analysis of
    Csokonai's poetry characterizing it as a search for escape from reality.
    Briefly considers also his two Debrecen friends.
JUHÁSZ, GÉZA. *Csokonai tanulmányok*. Edited by Izabella Juhász. Budapest:
    Akadémiai Kiadó, 1977. A collection of G. Juhász's essays on Csokonai,
    radically and militantly Marxist in their approach.
JULOW, VIKTOR. *Árkádia körül*. Budapest: Szépirodalmi Kiadó, 1975. A
    collection of excellent essays on literary life in Debrecen, most of them
    about Csokonai.
————. *Csokonai Vitéz Mihály*. Budapest: Gondolat, 1975. The most out-
    standing analysis of the poet's career with a great emphasis on the early
    Debrecen years.
PUNKÁNSZKYNÉ KÁDÁR, JOLÁN. *A drámaíró Csokonai*. Budapest: Akadémiai
    Kiadó, 1956. The first detailed analysis of Csokonai's dramas.
SINKÓ, ERVIN. *Csokonai életműve*. Novi Sad: Forum, 1965. A perceptive,
    detailed, and level-headed analysis of Csokonai's writings.
SZANA, TAMÁS. *Csokonai életrajza*. Debrecen és Nyiregyháza: Ifj. Csáthy
    Károly, 1869. The first biography by posterity.
SZAUDER, JÓZSEF. *Az estve és Az álom*. Felvilágosodás és klasszicizmus.

Budapest: Szépirodalmi Kiadó, 1970. An in-depth philological analysis of the process in which Csokonai's major philosophical poems developed from the early school exercises. The study concentrates on two poems and searches into the philosophical shaping forces behind those poems.

VARGHA, BALÁZS. *Csokonai Vitéz Mihály alkotásai és vallomásai tükrében.* Budapest: Szépirodalmi Kiadó, 1974. An attempt at finding answers to controversial issues in the poet's own writings and letters.

————, ed. *Csokonai emlékek.* Budapest: Akadémiai Kiadó, 1960. An indispensable collection of not easily available documents concerning the poet's life and career.

2. Articles

ADY, ENDRE. "Csokonai Vitéz Mihály." In *Költészet eś forradalom.* Budapest: Kossuth, 1969. An enlightening assessment by a fellow poet and former student of the College of Debrecen.

BARANY, GEORG. "Hope against Hope: The Enlightened Age in Hungary." *American Historical Review,* 76 (April–June, 1971), 319–57. An excellent analysis of the age and its poet.

BÁRCZY, KLÁRA. "Popular Tendency in the Works of Csokonai and Burns." *Hungarian Studies in English,* 9 (1975), 103–17. The first comparative study of the two poets.

BARÓTI, DEZSŐ. "CSOKONAI 'DOROTTYÁ'-ja." In *Írók, érzések, stílusok* Budapest: Magvető, 1971, pp. 204–39. A detailed analysis of Csokonai's mock-epic emphasizing its social aspects.

CUSHING, G. F. "The Birth of National Literature in Hungary." *Slavonic and East European Review,* 38 (December–June, 1959–1960), 458–75. The only in-depth study of the topic in English.

"Csokonai emlékszám." *Alföld,* 24, no. 11 (1973). A series of commemorative articles, written mostly by poets.

JULOW, VIKTOR. "A felvilágosodás és népiesség." In *A magyar irodalom törté-nete,* edited by Pál Pándi, III, 213–46. Budapest: Akadémiai Kiadó, 1965. A perceptive and informative interpretation of the poet's career.

————. "Csokonai klasszicizmusa és manierizmusa." *Alföld,* 24, no. 11 (1973), 71–84. The best analysis of the poet's various styles.

KISS, TAMÁS. "Csokonai két évszázada." In *Árkádiában éltünk.* Budapest: Szépirodalmi Kiadó, 1975. A most readable essay by one of Debrecen's contemporary poets.

MÓRICZ, ZSIGMOND. "Csokonai Vitéz Mihály." In *Válogatott irodalmi tanul-mányai.* Budapest: Művelt Nép, 1952. pp. 61–83. A sympathetic analysis by a fellow writer, also a former student of the College of Debrecen.

PÁNDI, PÁL. "Jegyzések Csokonai Vitéz Mihályról." *Csillag,* 4, no. 2 (1951), 219–39. A Marxist analysis of the poet's political attitudes.

————. "Csokonai Vitéz Mihály." In *A magyar irodalom története 1849-ig.* Budapest: Akadémiai Kiadó, 1964. pp. 254–69. A chapter outlining with

impeccable logic the official Marxist interpretation.
REMÉNYI, JÓZSEF. "Mihály Csokonai Vitéz." In *Three Hugarian Poets.*
Washington, D. C. 1955. pp. 47–64. A brief outline of the poet's career.
SŐTÉR, ISTVÁN. "Csokonai," "Csokonai alkotó módszere," "Csokonairól
olyanoknak, akik nem ismerhetik." In *Wertertől Szilveszterig.* Bu-
dapest: Szépirodalmi Kiadó, 1976, pp. 185–214. An invaluable compar-
atist study, establishing Csokonai's place in world literature.
SZERB, ANTAL. "Csokonai Vitéz Mihály." In *Magyar irodalomtörténet.*
Budapest: Magvető, 1972. pp. 254–60. An excellent introduction to the
rococo, preromantic, and folkloristic elements in Csokonai's poetry.
WALDAPFEL, IMRE. "Az igazi Csokonai." *Irodalmi tanulmányok*, no. 1 (1949),
40–58. The first important essay applying Marxist methods.

Index

165